The Life and Times of Emile Zola

Also by F. W. J. Hemmings

The Russian Novel in France 1884–1914
Emile Zola
Stendhal
Balzac: An Interpretation of la Comédie Humaine
Culture and Society in France 1848–1898
The Age of Realism

The Life and Times of

EMILE ZOLA

F.W.J. Hemmings

Paul Elek London

Published in Great Britain 1977 by
Elek Books Ltd
54-58 Caledonian Road, London NI 9RN

ISBN 0 236 40055 X

Printed in Great Britain by
The Garden City Press Limited,
Letchworth, Hertfordshire SG6 IJS

Contents

List of Illustrations

Prefatory Note

My first book on Zola, published in 1953 and completely revised for a later edition in 1966, was primarily a critical study of the works of the great French novelist. The present book represents the fulfilment of a long-standing ambition on my part to write a life of Zola, using all the relevant material that scholars from many countries have brought to light in the past twenty-five years or so. The two books have therefore different aims and should be regarded as separate though complementary.

All translations of Zola's writings used in this book are my own.

F.W.J.H.
Leicester, January 1977

Acknowledgements

The publishers are grateful to the following for permission to reproduce illustrations:

Bibliothèque Nationale, Paris, *frontispiece* and *pages* 1, 2, 3, 5, 7, 9, 10, 11, 25, 26, 27, 31, 33, 34, 35, 36, 39, 42, 43, 44, 47, 48, 49, 51, 56, 60, 64, 65, 69

Musée Carnavelet, Paris (Collection Céard, photography Jean-Louis Charmet), *pages* 30, 38, 40, 41, 46, 68, 73

Fogg Art Museum, Cambridge, Massachusetts, *page* 18

Photographie Giraudon, *page* 32

Documentation Hachette, *page* 16

Musée du Jeu de Paume, Paris, *front jacket* and *pages* 14, 19, 20, 24, 52, 54

Musée du Louvre, Paris, *page* 13

Metropolitan Museum of Art, New York, *page* 53

Sao Paulo Museum of Art, *page* 35

Private Collections, *pages* 12, 17

Radio Times Hulton Picture Library, *pages* 23, 29

Victoria and Albert Museum, London, *page* 8

Roger Viollet, *pages* 21, 37, 50, 66, 67, 76

Dr F. Emile-Zola, *pages* 4, 6, 15, 22, 28, 45, 55, 57, 58, 59, 61, 62, 63, 70, 71, 72, 74, 75 and *back jacket*

Introduction

The second half of the nineteenth century was a golden age for the fiction writer in France. Thanks to earlier reforms in the educational system made by Louis-Philippe's energetic Prime Minister Guizot, a newly literate generation had come of age and was now avid for material to read. The era of prosperity ushered in by the upsurge of economic activity in the 1850s meant that the average French family had more money to spend on leisure pursuits and marginally more spare time to devote to them. The forms of mass entertainment familiar to us today—the cinema, radio and television broadcasts, cheap travel—lay far in the future. Apart from occasional visits to the theatre or circus, the men and women of this earlier age were wholly dependent on the story-teller for that nurturing of the imaginative faculties that has always been felt as a fundamental requirement by ordinary people in every era and in all civilizations.

This was the age when Zola lived and launched himself on his extraordinarily successful career. Like Dickens in England a generation earlier, he spoke to a mass audience through the medium of the periodical press, the magazine or newspaper; the fact that their novels first appeared as serial stories may partly account for the keen sense, which both writers shared, of the immediacy of their reading public, all agog for the next instalment. Notes made by Zola before he started writing *Germinal*: 'the middle-class reader must experience a shudder of dread',[1] or when he was working out the plot of *La Bête humaine*: 'I would like, as subject, a violent drama capable of giving nightmares to everyone in Paris'[2]—such statements could almost have been made by Dickens when he sat down to compose *Oliver Twist* or *The Mystery of Edwin Drood*. The drab, uneventful, and repressed lives led by the great majority of the reading public in those days stimulated a demand for strong emotions and exciting action, safely sublimated in the imagined scenes of the world of fiction.

It was no mere coincidence that both Dickens and Zola started their literary careers as journalists; for this was also the age when the newspaper changed from being an expensive information sheet and forum for serious political discussion and began catering for the middle-brow reader who took a greater interest in the gossip column. The *causeries* and *chroniques* (amusing essays and short stories) that Zola was writing for the popular press in the late 1860s correspond closely, in manner and subject matter, to the 'Sketches by Boz' that Dickens was contributing to the *Evening Chronicle* in the mid 1830s. Politically, too, both men could be described as anti-establishment progressives. When Zola first came up to

Paris, in his late teens, the political atmosphere was stifling, and editors needed to keep a close watch on what was printed in their papers; for the authorities, who drew their support from the business and property-owning community, had no wish to see a recurrence of the social upheaval that had followed the 1848 Revolution. In the late 1860s, however, a more liberal policy was introduced, and the earlier strict political censorship was relaxed. This was the moment when Zola emerged as a satirical commentator on the events of the day. The kind of article he was signing in the last two years of the Second Empire shows that he already counted among the more radical members of the republican party. Simultaneously, he was planning the major creative undertaking with which his name is now chiefly associated—the series of twenty interlinked novels entitled *Les Rougon-Macquart*—and planning it as a documented exposure of the financial scandals and abuses of power with which the republicans of the period had for years been taxing Napoleon III and his ministers.

The Republic, so impatiently awaited, was proclaimed at a critical moment on 4 September 1870, the Emperor having abdicated after the humiliating defeat of his armies at Sedan. In spite of its shaky beginnings, the Third Republic endured for the rest of Zola's lifetime and indeed, outlasting the European war that followed, was to survive until a new German invasion dealt it its death-blow almost exactly seventy years after its painful birth. Few, however, would have been prepared to predict so long a spell of parliamentary rule when the Republic was set up in the middle of the disastrous war with Prussia. During the remaining three decades of the century, there were recurrent fears of a right-wing *coup* or else of a new revolution on the left, similar to but conceivably more successful than the attempt in 1871 to set up a working-class Commune in Paris.

Absorbed by his literary work, Zola played no active part in the turbulent political life of the period, though the trend of certain of his novels—particularly *L'Assommoir*, *Germinal*, and the book he wrote about the Franco-Prussian War, *La Débâcle*—showed clearly enough where his sympathies lay. Only when he was close on his sixties, and universally recognized, if not revered, as the nation's leading man of letters, did he suddenly decide to take a public stand on an issue which, though ostensibly turning on a suspected miscarriage of justice, had indisputable political implications. Zola's unexpected boldness in attempting to reopen the case of Captain Dreyfus, found formally guilty of military espionage and serving a life sentence in a penal colony overseas, was such as to place him at the focal point of world attention for months afterwards. His earlier, vaguely suspect reputation as the author of best-selling but somewhat unhallowed novels paled now before his new image as the lonely and courageous champion of a hapless victim of militarism and religious bigotry.

In his own country, this was not at all how Zola was seen except by an enlightened minority. His attack on the legality of the verdict passed on Dreyfus in 1894 aroused such a storm as had hardly been witnessed in France before. Zola was put on trial in his turn—a consequence he had foreseen and calmly discounted—and was eventually compelled to seek asylum abroad. The forces arrayed against him were the same as he had attacked in his writings all his life: obscurantism, authoritarianism, religious and racial prejudice. Though no intellectual in the narrow sense, Zola cherished an invincible belief in the power of reason and in the need to consolidate the achievements of the Enlightenment; in many respects, indeed, he was a true heir of the *encyclopédistes* of the eighteenth century who had waged unremitting warfare against the Roman Catholic Church and had helped lay the ideological foundations of the French Revolution. His slogans were, it is true, different from theirs: not Liberty, Equality, and Fraternity, but Truth and Justice; these two watchwords provided the titles for his last two novels, *Vérité*, which he wrote just before his death and which was published posthumously, and *Justice*, which he planned as its sequel but of which nothing has come down to us except the title itself and a few scrappy notes.

Justice and Truth can be interpreted as, respectively, the socio-political and the scientific aspects of the same basic imperative. Zola's lifelong faith in the power of science to banish not just ignorance and poverty but also cruelty and human degradation may appear naïve today, but in the context of his own time it was more understandable. People in the nineteenth century were far more aware of the positive achievements of science than of its potential menace. For thinking men, these achievements lay principally in a steadily increasing understanding of the workings of the universe; the masses were more impressed by the fruits of the new technology fathered by the physical sciences. The revolution in communications represented by the development of the railway and the steamship was already in full swing when Zola was born; his father, who began his working life as a railway construction engineer, had contributed to it in some small measure and the son, later on, in his novel *La Bête humaine*, explored many of the implications, moral as well as social, of the immeasurably speedier facilities for travel and transportation afforded by the railway engine. But the application of steam power to locomotion was only a beginning. Throughout Zola's life new products of applied science were forcing themselves on public attention one after the other, as electric lighting started to replace gas jets in the streets and oil lamps in houses, as the discovery of electric telegraphy led to the invention of the telephone, as the invention of the internal combusion engine resulted in the appearance on the roads of the first motor-cars, as the use of steel in construction work was given triumphal consecration in the shape of that novel landmark, the Eiffel Tower, and as progressive improvements in photography since the days of Niepce and Daguerre culminated in the first public moving-picture shows at the turn of the century.

None of these inventions fascinated Zola more than that of the hand-camera. He started experimenting with photography in his late forties, and throughout the rest of his life he took hundreds of high-quality pictures, of which a select sample can be studied in the pages of this book. His interest in the device derived from the same deep-seated bias towards the observation and reproduction of all aspects of the visible world which had been a permanent feature of his literary work almost from the start. Once the theoretical accretions have been stripped away, Zola's realism—his naturalism, to use the word he preferred—can be formulated as the literary correlative of the acute sense he possessed of the power of man's environment to mould his nature and his destiny. The human environment, which a writer may record on the printed page, can of course be fixed on the photographic plate or it can be transposed by the landscape painter working at his easel.

The very close relationship known to have existed between Zola and the Impressionist painters is not entirely attributable to the lucky chance that made Paul Cézanne his closest friend and confidant when the two of them were boys together at school in Aix-en-Provence. When Zola got to know Manet's work, and saw the open-air painting that Pissarro, Monet, and Renoir, among others, were experimenting with in the years immediately preceding the Franco-Prussian War, what struck him most and made him an ardent and eloquent convert to their art was the obvious truth that, like him, they were men aware of and enchanted by the spectacle of the external world. What they sought to represent was not nature and humanity as seen and represented by other men in past ages, but nature and humanity seen through their own eyes: colourful, vivid, often cheerful, sometimes mournful, occasionally grim. The fact that there was more to Impressionism than just this was not immediately apparent to Zola; for him the Impressionists were Naturalists, and therefore his brothers-in-arms.

But Impressionism was, of course, only a passing phase in the rapidly evolving pageant of French art. So too was Naturalism in the shifting kaleidoscope of French literature, a fact that Zola came to recognize implicitly though he may never have gone so far as to acknowledge it publicly. His best novels, those for which he is now and always will be remembered, are much more than impressionistic frescoes of a social scene now long vanished. They are tinged with unearthly colours, they are imbued with a murky ferocity and a doom-laden *Angst*, which owe little to the surface appearance of things and a great deal to the underlying neuroses of his own tormented spirit and to the buried stresses of that volcanic age in which he lived his life.

1 Father and Son

A visitor to Paris today, leaving the Métro at the Bourse station by the north-east exit, needs only to walk a short distance before entering a certain narrow street running between the Rue Montmartre and the Rue du Sentier. A grimy plaque on a house at the far end will inform him that this was the exact spot where Emile Zola was born in 1840. The street bears the same name as it did then, Rue St Joseph, but in former times, so Zola remembered being told, it was known as the Rue du Temps perdu. Providence is not always as apt as it is supposed proverbially to be; one does not need to cudgel one's brains to think of a novelist for whom a street so designated would have been a far more appropriate birthplace. To Zola, in later years, the old name suggested nothing more than the rather trite idea that 'time was very valuable and ought never to be lost, or wasted'.[1]

1 Zola's birthplace, 10 Rue St Joseph, Paris

According to another family tradition, the house itself had been built over a disused graveyard which had once held the mortal remains of Molière and La Fontaine. But a more relevant omen lay in the fact that the district in which the Rue St Joseph was situated harboured most of the newspaper printing offices of the capital. It was the Paris equivalent to Fleet Street, and the rumble of the rotary presses running off the morning editions may well have been distantly audible in the third-storey room at No. 10 where,

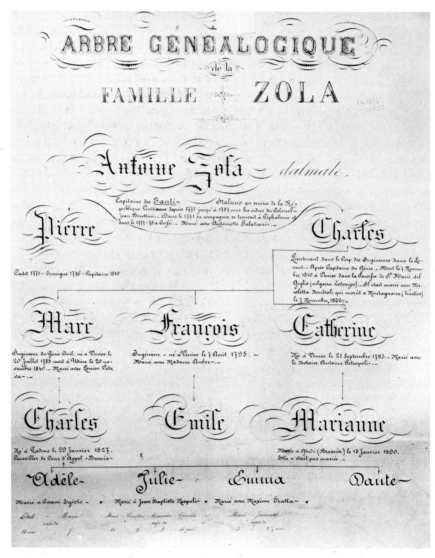

2 A family tree drawn up on Zola's instructions in 1894. At that time his only surviving relatives on his father's side were Carlo (Charles) and his children

at eleven in the evening on 2 April 1840, the young married woman—she had had her twenty-first birthday only three weeks previously—was brought to bed of a boy, her first and, as it turned out, her only child.

Emile Zola's mother was of humble birth. Her family, surnamed Aubert, had been settled at Dourdan, a small town about thirty miles from Paris in the direction of Chartres, since at least the beginning of the century. Her father was a glazier, her mother, before she married, a sempstress. Some time in the early 1830s the family, consisting of her parents and three elder brothers beside herself, joined the flow of working-class immigrants who under the July Monarchy were leaving the nearby country districts in great numbers to settle in Paris. Here the Auberts seem to have prospered, relatively speaking, but even so, the fact that their daughter Emilie should have married as well as she did must have seemed to them little short of wonderful. Clearly her father was in no position to dower her, and it must have been her plump good looks alone that won the heart of the forty-four-year-old Francesco Zola when he saw her leaving church after mass one Sunday morning. For the Auberts, this foreigner with the high forehead and long nose with its oddly cleft tip—both features that he transmitted to his son—would have seemed a real gentleman, a *monsieur*. How he touched Emilie's heart we do not know; possibly his exotic origins and the stories he had to tell of his adventurous past life helped her to forget the difference in age. In any case, it was by no means uncommon in those days for men to settle down in their maturity with brides young enough to be their daughters.

Zola's father was born a citizen of the ancient Republic of Venice, though he was still an infant when, by the treaty of Campo-Formio, Napoleon Bonaparte extinguished the city's independence and handed its territory over to the Emperor of Austria. The Zolas were a distinguished military family: Francesco's father, his two uncles, and his paternal grandfather had all served in the Venetian forces. Following in the family tradition, the young man enlisted in the Austro-Italian army and simultaneously enrolled as a student of mathematics at Padua University. His doctoral thesis, which had to do with the art of surveying, was published in 1818 and became a standard textbook in Milan for civil engineers.

In 1820 he resigned his commission and went into partnership with his brother Marco who was running a construction business. Five years later he joined the team of experts planning the first public railway on the continent of Europe: a track to be laid through difficult country—wooded, swampy, and very hilly in parts—from the Bohemian town of Budweis (modern Ceske Budejovice) to the Upper Austrian city of Linz. The purpose was to facilitate the transport of commodities, in particular salt, between the Danube and the navigable lower stretch of the River Vltava, which flows north to Prague. Each train of wagons was to be pulled by two drayhorses, harnessed one behind the other, for steam engines were still not thought of at this date, or not, at least, in the Austrian Empire.

3 La Canebière, Marseilles, with the Vieux Port in the background, as it appeared when Francesco Zola opened his office there in 1832

It is some evidence of Francesco Zola's grasp of practical matters that, even before this line was opened, he was privately planning its extension south from Linz to Gmunden on the Traunsee, near where the salt-mines of the Salzkammergut were situated. In 1829 he applied for and was granted a concession for this undertaking. But although the new railway was eventually built (between 1834 and 1836), Francesco who had pioneered it had no hand in its construction. This may have been because of unforeseen difficulties in securing financial backing: with the sniff of revolution in the air, it was not a good moment to coax money out of bankers and businessmen. Or there may have been a different reason. Emile Zola always believed that after leaving Austria his father spent some time in England. Now Francesco's chief, the gifted German-Czech engineer Anton von Gerstner, who had planned and supervised the original Budweis–Linz line, had even before its completion fallen out with the company shareholders over the question whether the railway should be built with gradients and curves of a nature to permit eventual conversion to steam traction. Having failed to persuade his backers to allow him to do this, Gerstner resigned his position and left for England. There is a bare possibility that he took his young Venetian associate with him to examine at first hand the progress made, in the native land of steam locomotive transport, since the opening of the Stockton–Darlington line in 1825.

If Francesco did cross the Channel, his stay in Great Britain cannot have lasted long, since we pick up his trace again in Paris at the end of 1830 when he volunteered for service in the newly constituted Foreign Legion, which had been formed to assist in the French conquest of Algeria. But this second spell of military service was brief and inglorious; it came to a sudden end when he found himself obliged to resign his commission in consequence of some trouble arising out of an entanglement with the too-alluring wife of a German sergeant in the Legion.

He then decided to resume his previous calling and began practising as a civil engineer in Marseilles. Within two years he had his own office on the Canebière and was employing a small staff of draughtsmen and apprentices. This was an age of opportunity for clever and enterprising engineers. Large-scale projects such as cutting a canal through the Isthmus of Suez, tunnelling under the English Channel and beneath the capital cities of Europe to lay underground railways, were already being dreamed of by men who combined vision with practical experience; Francesco Zola was one of these, though his own schemes were rather less grandiose than those instanced. It was his great misfortune that none of them came to fruition during his lifetime. Pioneering work of this kind depended for its successful accomplishment on the co-operation and good will of a great many people whose interests had, one way or another, to be harmonized. In enlisting support, in dealing with objectors, in worsting unscrupulous business competitors, Francesco displayed energy, patience, and skill. Though French was not his native language, he had the knack of using it to express his ideas and press home his arguments with eloquence and even with a certain stylistic verve, as his extant correspondence and published pamphlets demonstrate. Yet with all this talent—mechanical, commercial, linguistic, diplomatic—the fact remains that he never succeeded in reaping the fruit of his labours. This failure, due to ill luck rather than lack of persistence, may well have impressed his son more than any of the incidental achievements of his father's career, and may have obscurely prompted him to choose a different avocation, one in which results depended on personal endeavour alone. If Emile became, when he grew up, a lone fighter, was this not because his father's efforts to establish himself as a captain of men had met with such uncertain success?

At Marseilles, the first large-scale operation for which Francesco Zola attempted to win a contract was to supply the city with gaslight for its principal thoroughfares. This novel mode of illumination had already been tried in Paris, and was to be brought to Marseilles a few years later; but the Italian engineer was ahead of his time. Almost immediately, he was taken with a new idea, one that was to preoccupy him for most of the rest of his life. With the opening up of North Africa to French trade, the port of Marseilles was being more heavily used than ever before. The natural harbour it possessed, one of the safest anchorages in the West

Mediterranean, had served it well since the distant days when the Phoenicians and the Greeks discovered its advantages; but this harbour, the so-called Vieux Port, was now too small for the increased traffic. Moreover, it was dangerous for sailing-ships to try and leave when the strong north-westerlies were blowing, as they were apt to for long periods of the year. Zola's project was essentially to retain the Vieux Port as the home dock, but to connect it by means of a canal running behind the Corniche to a new dockyard down the coast, in the inlet known by the picturesque name of the Anse de la Fausse Monnaie (Coiners' Cove).

He battled for this idea for years. His plan got as far as being seriously considered in Paris, for the extension of the dockyards at Marseilles was as much a matter of national as of local interest. He had an audience with Louis-Philippe and another, in 1836, with one of his sons, the Prince de Joinville, whose name he intended to give to the new docks. The official *Moniteur universel*, reporting this interview, noted that the young prince displayed a marked interest not only in the blueprint for the canal and dock but also in the 'highly ingenious mechanical devices invented by M. Zola in order to render the execution of this project more rapid and less costly'.[2] The newspaper did not divulge details of these 'highly ingenious devices', but the reference reminds us that Francesco Zola was not just a surveying engineer; he possessed an inventive streak as well, as was shown again some years later when he took out a patent for an earth-moving machine, which was used in the erection of fortifications on the north side of Paris, at Clignancourt.

Three and a half years after this royal audience, the issue still hung in the balance. A letter written at the beginning of 1839 to his sister Caterina in Italy shows Francesco in an optimistic frame of mind, worried about his immediate financial situation but sensing, like the gambler he was, a huge prize within his grasp. All the investigating committees were satisfied; the government had approved the scheme and were prepared to give it financial backing; he was currently negotiating his fee, which he reckoned would be fixed at between 80,000 and 100,000 francs; but there was still no definite commitment on the part of the authorities, it was always jam tomorrow. 'In the meantime I have used up in four years all the money put by at Marseilles; I have spent three years in Paris without earning a penny and I have in addition incurred debts to the tune of 20,000 francs so as to obtain by all possible means the satisfactory conclusion of so important a piece of business.'[3] In the event it was all in vain: his chief commercial rival, a certain Eugène Flachat, succeeded in wresting the commission from him and the new port at Marseilles, the Bassin de la Joliette, was constructed to the north of the Vieux Port in accordance with a totally different plan.

4 Painting of Francesco and Emilie Zola, with Emile, executed in 1845 (artist unknown)

It was when his affairs were at this crisis that Francesco, as we have seen, married after a whirlwind courtship. Fortunately he had other irons in the fire. A less ambitious scheme than the Marseilles dock project had occurred to him some six months before he made Emilie his wife; this was to build a dam near Le Tholonet, at the opening of the Infernat gorges in the mountainous region above Aix-en-Provence, and to channel the waters collected behind the dam down into the city. The old provincial capital, famous today for its numerous public fountains, suffered in those times from a chronic shortage of water, as too did the surrounding countryside; it was part of Zola's scheme to irrigate the arid fields by a system of ditches tapping the water from his canal.

As before, he was successful in securing the backing of the men at the top, including the leading statesman Thiers, who had a great deal of pull at Aix. But, once again, negotiations were protracted, largely on account of the greed of the local landowners, whose inflated demands for compensation meant that although royal approval for the canal project was forthcoming in 1844, nearly three more years elapsed before work could begin. Moving from Aix to Paris and back with his family, Francesco continued to plot, argue, solicit, petition, living all the time on borrowed money, and raising yet more capital to finance the enterprise. In midsummer 1846 a joint-stock company, the Société du Canal Zola, was floated and Francesco, as managing director, returned to Aix to start active operations. While supervising his workmen in the mountains he caught a chill, but chose to disregard the infection and travelled on to Marseilles where he had urgent business to see to. Here he fell seriously ill; pleurisy was diagnosed, his young wife was sent for, and arrived in time to watch him die in a dingy hotel room, while the careless shouts of the travellers and ostlers rose from the courtyard below.

2 Aix-en-Provence

Francesco's death occurred less than a week before Emile's seventh birthday, and the funeral, which took place at Aix, was almost the only personal memory that he conserved of the brilliant but erratic adventurer who was his father. Towards the end of his own life he described the occasion and the pathetic image he retained of himself as 'a pale little lad, walking at the head of the long procession, through the streets crowded with people who had come to pay their last respects to the remains of their benefactor'.[1]

His paleness may have been only partly due to the solemnity of the occasion and a precocious sense of the magnitude of his bereavement. Pampered by his fond parents in his early years, he seems to have grown up a somewhat sickly child, and this may have been one reason why the young widow decided to give up the big house in the Impasse Sylvacanne where they had been living and move into the country, to the nearby hamlet of Pont-de-Béraud. The other reason was to save money. Francesco's death had left Emilie in difficult circumstances. All he had apparently done to secure her future and that of their child was to take the necessary legal steps to relieve her of liability for his debts. The only assets he left were the 172 shares in the company he had founded, which would have entitled him to one-twelfth of the profits once the canal was operating. Over the ensuing years his creditors and the other major shareholders managed to strip her of any rights she might have had in the Canal Company. Rash attempts to secure redress in the courts only worsened the situation, and in 1858, when Zola was just eighteen, she decided to cut her losses, shake the dust of Aix from her feet and, as a last desperate resort, go and see whether any of her husband's former friends and connections in Paris could help her.

In later life, Zola seldom had a good word to say for Aix. 'An old capital city, living on its memories, with nothing to commend it but the beauty of its skies';[2] 'Aix, frozen in the arrogant airs it gives itself as a former capital city, with no industry, nothing but a law faculty which it has been allowed to keep as consolation for the loss of its one-time greatness';[3] such disdainful remarks are typical of the references he made in the Paris press to the town where he spent his childhood and where he was brought up. But these judgements are distorted by the animosity he felt towards those citizens of Aix who had despoiled his widowed mother and robbed him of his inheritance. The truth is that his attitude was ambivalent, being founded on a mixture of happy and painful memories.

5 A satirical reference, in a contemporary cartoon, to the plight of investors in the Canal Company after Francesco Zola's death

Parts of the sleepy old town always retained for him a kind of magic charm. There was the ancient, disused cemetery where he played as a small urchin and which he evokes in the opening pages of *La Fortune des Rougon*, with its tall, rank grass and the gnarled old pear trees, rooted in a soil enriched by decaying corpses, which bore enormous pears. 'In the town, people talked of these fruits with grimaces of disgust; but the local boys had no such qualms, and every evening, at dusk, gangs of them would scale the walls to steal the pears even before they were properly ripe.'[4] When Emile was eleven years old the cemetery was cleared to make room for an extension of the hydropathic establishment, and he almost certainly remembered—since he mentions it in the same novel—the scandal caused by the negligent way the sexton tossed the disinterred bones into a filthy old cart drawn by a donkey, which he then drove in broad daylight through the cobbled streets, followed by a crowd of whooping boys. Every now and then a skull bounced off from the top of the heap, and was immediately snatched up and carried off to be used by the godless ragamuffins in a ghoulish game of bowls.

In the same area, but a little further out, there existed at the time a strip of common land on which gipsies had squatted from time immemorial. It was another favourite spot for the little Emile to visit, with his two friends Marius Roux and Philippe Solari, when they were playing truant from their preparatory school. The burghers of Aix looked askance at the gipsies, whom they accused of killing stray cats and dogs and putting them into the stew-pot; but the boys wandered freely around the encampment, peeping into the caravans and staring cheekily at the well-built, black-eyed Romany beauties who were conversing with one another in an incomprehensible jargon that was neither French nor Provençal.

He never forgot the excitement caused by the Crimean War; he was fourteen at the time. The troops riding down to the coast frequently halted overnight at Aix, and at crack of dawn the boys would be there to see them leave, the rising sun glinting on their weapons, on the buttons of their uniforms and the burnished metal of their helmets. Off they went, flags flying, bugles playing and drums beating, while the schoolboys ran along behind them, their satchels bumping on their backs. Greatly daring, they sometimes followed the soldiers as far as the next village down the road; then they would climb a hill 'and from that distant vantage-point, between the folds in the ground, along the winding road, we followed the regiment with our eyes, watching it grow smaller and finally disappear, with its numberless little fiery sparks, into the dazzling brightness of the horizon.'[5]

For the most part the citizens of Aix detested the military and scowled when the poor conscripts presented themselves with a billeting order. But the Zolas—perhaps out of respect for Francesco, twice a soldier during his lifetime—always found room for them. Old Mme Aubert, Emile's grand-mother, welcomed them in, sat them down at the kitchen table, and made them tell her where they came from; and if one of them happened to hail from her native Beauce she would cook him something good, something that did not have the taste of the eternal olive oil she could never get accustomed to even after years of living in the south. A few who came back that way called in to see her again; but many never returned, and those who did were only too often pale, shaking with fever or limping from a gunshot wound.

One adventure, which it is not possible to date as precisely, but which left a deep impression on Emile, took place outside Aix. In the course of a solitary ramble along the banks of the Durance, on a baking afternoon in July, his way took him past a long stone wall behind which grew tall forest trees curtaining off whatever lay beyond. Skirting the brambles and thistles that grew rankly at its base, he finally found a gap in the wall and scrambled through. Inside it was cool, the stridulation of the cicadas could no longer be heard, only, occasionally, the cry of a bird high up in the tree-tops. He struggled through the undergrowth till he came to a glade and could just make out a straight path leading off through the gloom; scuffing the moss with his feet, he discovered cobble-stones underneath. The ivy was monstrously thick on the tree trunks, creepers caught at his face as he passed; crouching every now and then, he walked on, his heart beating, and came at last to a wide clearing. He could see what had been trim box-hedges, which no gardener had taken his shears to for half a century perhaps; the rambler roses rioted over them, releasing their heavy scent on the oppressively still air. In the crevices of the garden steps grew gillyflowers, and flowering bushes he had never seen before had rooted themselves in the dried ponds. Beyond a crumbling stone balustrade rose the walls and broken windows of a ruinous pavilion. Not daring to make his way inside, he crept round, attracted by a sound of dripping water. In the centre of an ornamental lake, with huge water-lilies spread over its surface, a fountain still played, while beside it stood a stone Cupid green with moss. A gust of wind, suddenly parting the foliage, let through a flickering sunbeam, and gave him a momentary, illusory impression of a white-limbed girl disappearing behind the trunks of the trees that fringed the lake.

Emile kept quiet about his discovery and may never have revisited the deserted park, preferring to retain the enchantment of his first exploration. But the adventure took root in his imagination and emerged in different forms once his literary vocation had declared itself, though the setting is always the same, an overgrown, neglected pleasure-garden, and there is always the girl he fancied he had seen, pictured as a water-nymph in the story *Simplice*, which he published in 1863, as an adventurous young countess given to bathing by moonlight in another story written ten years later, and finally as Albine, the heroine of *La Faute de l'abbé Mouret* (1875), the novel in which the memory is given its most elaborate extension.

Normally, it was only during the summer holidays that day-long excursions such as that just described were feasible. Zola's regular schooling had started when he was twelve and was accepted as a boarder at the Collège d'Aix (Lycée Bourbon). His mother's diminishing resources could not have stretched to paying the fees and maintenance; fortunately, her dead husband's name still carried enough weight for his son to be awarded a bursary by the civic authorities.

The school was housed in a former convent, a great, rambling place built round three sides of a wide courtyard facing south, which was planted with magnificent plane-trees; in spring and summer the thousands of sparrows that nested there kept up a deafening twitter at dusk and at dawn. A second, smaller courtyard was separated from the larger by a bathing pool in which the pupils were allowed to take dips when the weather was warm enough; it was the only form of physical exercise

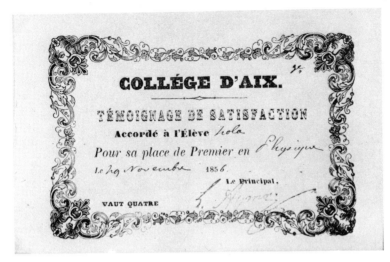

6 Zola comes first in physics. A certificate of this kind dispensed the holder from a stated number (four in this instance) of detention hours

provided for. The classrooms and dormitories were bare, whitewashed, unheated rooms, but the cold troubled the boys less than the appallingly bad food, served up in a rather splendid refectory with black marble tables. Certain dishes made young Emile's gorge rise every time they appeared: a certain rancid cod stew, or runner beans floating in a disgusting white sauce. Confronted with these horrors, he stilled his appetite by eating as much bread as he could and stuffing the remainder of the loaf into his pocket for future consumption. On one occasion at least the food was so bad that the boys rioted, throwing it, plates and all, at the head of the master detailed for dinner duty; then some of them barricaded themselves in, bawling the 'Marseillaise', and the gendarmerie had to be sent for to restore order. It all ended with the expulsion of five of the ringleaders and a very temporary amelioration in the quality of the school meals.

The intellectual fare offered was of a slightly higher order, but it was monotonous and restricted. The classical languages were the mainstay of the syllabus; no modern history was taught, nor any of the modern languages. English and German were despised as being of use only to such clods as intended to go into trade. All his life, Zola never knew any language but French. When he became famous and his Italian cousins tried to get in touch with him, he had to have their letters translated; and later still, as a political refugee in England, it was a major source of irritation to him that he could not even read the news about the progress of the Dreyfus Affair in the London papers. Even the literature of his own country and century might have remained a closed book to him until much later, had it not been for one unusually broad-minded teacher who

7 Cézanne evokes their schoolboy bathing exploits in the River Arc: sketch included in a letter to Zola

took them in the third form and got them to read the great poets of the romantic age, Lamartine, Hugo, and Musset.

Whether on balance Zola can be said to have been happy at school is not an easy question to decide. Certainly when he first entered the Collège d'Aix he found it hard to adapt to the new life, having had nothing but indulgent treatment at the hands of the two women, his mother and his grandmother, who had brought him up since the age of seven. His class-mates teased him for his slight lisp and what they called his Parisian accent, and perhaps went further than that: there was a good deal of quite cruel bullying to which the *pions*—impecunious students working their way through college whose job was to try and keep some sort of order among the boys—tended to turn a blind eye. But he settled down and must have worked hard, however little he enjoyed memorizing Latin declensions and conjugations, since his name figures frequently among the prize-winners. Even at this age, it is probable he realized how much depended on him, as the future head of the household, and how important it was that he should get a footing on the career ladder as soon as he could. And in spite of the cold in winter, the constant pangs of hunger, the rowdyism, the dirt and bad smells, the droning teachers, and the lack of freedom, there were compensations: the forbidden novels read in class behind an open dictionary propped up on the desk; his first pipe, however much it made him retch; and his first attempts at creative writing, mostly short sketches about school life in dramatic form, of which nothing has come down to us but the titles.

Also, he had his confidants and bosom friends, two in particular, Paul Cézanne and Baptistin Baille. The latter became a teacher in the Ecole Polytechnique and drifted away from the other two some time before the Franco-Prussian War; the friendship between Zola and Cézanne lasted much longer, until they were in their mid-forties in fact, and we shall have occasion to revert to it more than once. At this stage Cézanne's vocation was only just beginning to declare itself; he shared all Zola's juvenile enthusiasm for the romantic poets, while Zola was as keen on painting and sketching as his friend—in fact it was Zola, not Cézanne, who used to win the school prize for drawing.

The trio differed from most other boys of their age at Aix, who tended to while away their leisure hours sitting in cafés over endless card-games; they were, all three, fresh-air fiends. Whenever they had a day off, they would leave the town and make their way up the Arc, a river shallow enough in summer to be crossed on stepping-stones, but concealing here and there deep pools, called *goures* in the local dialect, which were ideal for bathing. All three were practised swimmers. When not actually in the water, they would lie around on the sandy soil, shying stones at random targets, catching frogs and searching for eels. In November, when it grew too cold for such amusements, they would set out before dawn with a gun in one hand and a few caged birds strung on a pole in the other. Up in the hills, they made a halt at one of the typical hunter's hides, a squat, cylindrical structure half buried in the ground, with slits for the guns. The bird-cages were hung on the branches of a convenient tree, and when some unwary thrush, lured by the warbling of the captive, settled near a cage, the hunter would align his sights and pull the trigger. Usually the thrush flew off unharmed, especially if Zola was the marksman; at fifteen, he was already a little short-sighted.

In the summer months, the guns they carried were for show only. The bag would rarely amount to more than a couple of sparrows, or an even more inedible bat that one of them had let fly at, for fun, as they returned home in the dusk. The real objective of these rambles was to see how far they could get, in this countryside of rocks, pines, and scattered olive groves. They dreamed of a Huckleberry Finn existence, camping out on the banks of the Arc a whole summer. When they grew tired of discussing the *pions* and mimicking the masters, they would act out one of Hugo's verse dramas, Cézanne making his voice squeak when he had the part of Doña Sol or the Queen of Spain; or else Zola would recite long passages from Musset's melancholy rhapsodies, *Rolla* or *Les Nuits*.

Such poetry, embodying the railings of a suicidal libertine or the lamentations of the deceived and disappointed lover, represented the pure essence of the romantic *mal du siècle*. But it was harmless enough in its effects: for Zola and his friends, Musset's verses acted as a surrogate for the passions they had never experienced, rather than an incitement to seek some object for their as yet unaroused instincts. Certainly it was a far cry from the poet's lurid scenarios to the first, timid stirrings of tenderness that Zola felt for the young girl he calls Gratienne in one of the earliest pieces of verse he wrote ('A mes Amis', dated 1858) and to whom he later referred, in a few of the letters he wrote to Baille from Paris, as 'l'Aérienne'. In one of them he tells how, walking in the Jardin des Plantes one day, he chanced to see a girl who reminded him of 'l'Aérienne' and this started him wondering why he had not pressed his suit a little more confidently; ought he not at least to have written her a letter, offering her his friendship? Baille replied telling him his Dulcinea had taken a lover, but Zola pretended to be unaffected by the news. 'It was not with S . . . that I was in love, and still am perhaps; it was with "l'Aérienne", an ideal creature whom I did not so much see as dream of.'[6] Imagination, and the reveries of an introspective nature, contributed more, certainly, to his baffled yearning than did crude adolescent sexual drive.

Who the object of his affections was, no one knows for certain, but such evidence as we have points fairly strongly in one direction. Many years later, when Zola was a middle-aged married man, a curious story appeared in an illustrated magazine under the heading 'Emile Zola's first romance'. It attracted some attention, since by this time (1887) Zola was at the height of his fame as a novelist; the story was even translated into English and published in Chicago as a five-cent paperback. Unless we postulate an indiscretion on the part of Cézanne or someone else who had known him as a boy at Aix, we must suppose that Zola himself provided the journalist with his material, in which case many details, including the name the girl is given (Jeanne) may have been deliberately altered to camouflage the truth. The one episode in the idyll that seems to ring true concerns an afternoon that he spent with her in her parents' garden. Too shy to put his feelings into words, or even to find anything at all to say, the timid adolescent kept picking bunches of grapes for her until finally, having eaten as much as she could, she thanked him gravely and went indoors.

The illustrations accompanying the article included a portrait of 'Jeanne' in a circular frame. Under the bonnet—a pink bonnet, according to the story—a pigtail of black hair can be seen snaking over one shoulder, while heavy tresses fall across her forehead. The nose is straight, the lips are full and slightly pouted. It may not be pure chance that this lithograph bears a striking resemblance to a medallion known to have been presented to Zola by the sculptor Philippe Solari, who had been at school with him in Aix. Now Philippe had a sister called Louise; could it be that the medallion represents her and that Philippe gave it to Zola because he knew his friend had once been deeply attached to her? Louise Solari was, it is true, a good deal younger than Zola; in fact, she would hardly have been in her teens when he left Aix for Paris, which might seem to rule out the possibility that he could have felt for her the kind of ethereal adoration he expresses when speaking of 'l'Aérienne'. But if we look at the first volume of the *Rougon-Macquart* series we find that the heroine, Miette Chantegreil, is only thirteen, and that the age-gap between her and Silvère Mouret, the hero of the novel, is almost exactly that between Louise Solari and Zola himself. In the opening chapter of *La Fortune des Rougon* the narrator describes Miette as 'a child, but a child on the verge of womanhood . . . thanks to the climate and the active life she led'. He dwells with particular attention on her 'superb head of hair; springing thick and straight from her forehead, it was tossed vigorously back, like a rising wave, and flowed over her head and neck in a sea of curls, full of capricious eddies, as black as ink.'[7]

If any doubts remain, a note Zola made about Miette when he was drafting *La Fortune des Rougon* seems to settle the issue. This note ends as follows: 'a good-looking, sturdy girl; round face, black wavy hair falling low over her forehead, lips rather thick and red. Peasant dress. (Louise Solari).'[8]

8 An illustration of the girl who was probably Louise Solari, from *La Revue Illustrée*, 1887

3 Lost Illusions

Zola's carefree boyhood came to an end in February 1858 when his mother, who had travelled up to Paris at the end of the previous year, wrote telling him to sell what few chattels they had left, the proceeds of which should cover his fare from Aix and that of his grandfather. His grandmother, the sturdy old peasant woman whose cheerfulness had helped keep up her daughter's spirits during the difficult first years of her widowhood, had died in November. Emilie's protracted legal tussle with the directors of the Canal Company had ended in defeat. The only hope now was that the few well-placed friends left to them in Paris would come to their assistance.

She had made one earlier attempt to contact them and seek their advice. This was in 1851, when Emile had just turned eleven; they had stayed for six months with her married brother, Adolphe Aubert, a house-painter, frequently unemployed, who had a daughter, Anna, of Emile's age. It is likely that this earlier visit left him with a clearer memory of this pretty little cousin than of the capital itself. But in 1858, in his eighteenth year, he was more sensitive to the appearance and atmosphere of his native city, a city he hardly knew. His first impression, as the stage-coach trundled up through the spoiled suburbs of Montrouge and Arcueil, was overwhelmingly depressing. It was a treeless landscape of worked-out quarries; the great wheels of the winches, silhouetted against the horizon, made the young traveller think of gibbets and guillotines. Otherwise there was nothing to be seen but tumbledown hovels and mounds of industrial waste. The coach swayed as the wheels sank into the ruts, and round a bend in the road he saw a trembling old horse, tied to a post, sniffing out the meagre tufts of grass that grew in the chalky soil. His arrival in Paris was, he later recalled, 'one of the cruellest disappointments in my life. I was expecting a row of palaces, but for close on a league the heavy vehicle passed between sinister looking buildings, taverns and thieves' dens, a whole slum lining the road. Then we threaded our way between ill-lit streets. Paris seemed more constricted and gloomy than the small town we had come from.'[1]

What Zola found was a city ringing to the sound of sledge-hammers and pickaxes, as Baron Haussmann's demolition men moved across it. The master-plan to bring up to date the internal communication system of Paris was now being implemented, regardless of cost and regardless of the temporary inconvenience incurred by certain classes of citizen. The eventual outcome was a more orderly, more airy, and more handsome

9 Old houses being pulled down as part of the programme to renovate the capital which was in full swing when Zola arrived in Paris in 1858

capital city, but in the meantime, as old houses were pulled down in their hundreds to make room for the new, wide boulevards, overcrowding, which had been a menace for generations, grew worse, and the single tenement house (No. 63) in the Rue Monsieur-le-Prince, where his mother gave him and his grandfather a worried welcome, was in fact divided up into no fewer than fifty minute apartments. As the pressure on living-space increased, new storeys had been added to these old houses; courtyards and gardens had been built over, while extensions here and there encroached on the sidewalks of the already narrow streets. Paris was dark, noisy, and smelly too, the streets slippery with horse droppings and refuse of the foulest kind. Little wonder that Emile felt violently homesick for the sweet scent of thyme and lavender that perfumed the countryside round Aix.

His mother's first concern was quite properly with his education. One of the few influential people she could still approach was Maître Labot, *avocat au Conseil d'Etat*, who had known her husband well and had in fact pronounced the traditional oration at his graveside. Labot spoke to his friend Désiré Nisard, a noted literary historian and at the time director of the Ecole Normale Supérieure, with the result that Emile was awarded a bursary to enable him to attend one of the oldest and most prestigious schools in Paris.

At the Lycée Bourbon in Aix Zola had been one of the prize-winners; here, at the Lycée Saint-Louis, his position was a little like that of an English grammar-school boy before the war who had won an open exhibition to one of the ancient universities. He found himself, in other words, ill at ease, overawed by his fellow students, awkwardly conscious of his regional accent. All his class-mates seemed so self-assured; even the circles they drew on the blackboard during geometry lessons had a perfection of form he could not emulate. Their fluency in discussing all the latest plays was matched only by the aplomb with which they flourished the photographs of actresses they kept tucked into their pocket-books; photographs, the latest novelty! They read the papers, were well up on current affairs, and one or two of them had got hold of copies of *Madame Bovary*, the pornographic novel that had been at the centre of a notorious court case the year before.

They were far too elegant, far too sophisticated for Zola to make friends of any of them. He poured out his loneliness in long letters to Baille and Cézanne back in Aix. His discouragement was such that he stopped working seriously, and none of his teachers took any notice. With classes of sixty, they never troubled themselves about those who were not keeping up. Only one member of the staff of the Lycée Saint-Louis made any impression on Zola; this was Pierre-Emile Levasseur, who had been a fellow student of Taine's at the Ecole Normale. He taught literature and composition, and Zola's one hour of triumph was when Levasseur read out to the class an essay he had written on Milton.

Seeing how the boy was pining for former haunts, his mother consented to let him spend the summer holidays in Aix. On his return he succumbed to an attack of what was called in those days brain fever, and was for a while delirious. It was the only serious illness Zola ever had, though as we shall see he was subject later on to fits of nervous depression bad enough to keep him in bed for several days. The dreams he had when this fever was at its height remained obsessively in his memory and some years later he wrote down what he could remember of them, for possible use in one of his novels, everything being grist to a writer's mill. He imagined himself underground, moving along narrow, low-ceilinged galleries. Roots he could not see dragged at his legs; he had constantly to use his hands to push away heaps of debris while his knees, as he crawled along, sank into the sticky ground. Sometimes the tunnel would grow narrower so that he could hardly squeeze through, at other times he was up to his waist in gelatinous sludge, or clambering painfully over huge stone-falls. But he could never pause; always he had to press on, to make his way out, to arrive. 'Arrive where? I had no idea. Perhaps I had some vague intuition that, if ever I could get to the end of the endless tunnel, I should see before me some vast horizon, limpid and serene.'[2]

Today we would interpret this dream in terms of birth-symbolism. Zola, who never had the chance to study Freud, drew an analogy with the germinating seedling struggling in the springtime up through the wet or stony ground into the light of day, and this may have suggested to him the idea of giving his novel about miners, a large part of which describes men struggling through just such dark, narrow, and obstructed galleries as he dreamed of in his fever, the title *Germinal*.

In spite of missing through illness the first two months of the new academic year, Zola passed the written part of the school-leaving examination, the *baccalauréat*, with ease; but when it came to the oral he went to pieces, and mixed up Charlemagne and Saint Louis. He made a second attempt in the summer of 1859, travelling down to Marseilles from Aix to sit the papers, but this time failed outright and was not even admitted to take the oral.

The good Labot, remembering his old friend Francesco, a laureate of the University of Padua, shook his head. But he exerted himself once more on the boy's behalf, and found him a situation as copy clerk in the Excise Office. From nine to four Zola transcribed entries into ledgers, read his newspaper, or listened to a fellow clerk reminiscing about his war experiences; what a relief to get out into the warm afternoon sunshine, light his pipe, and stroll home! After a couple of months he threw it up and decided to devote himself full time to writing. 'My dream', he told Baille, 'is to publish within two years from now two volumes, one of prose and one of verse. As for the future, who knows? If I definitely embark on a literary career, I shall be true to my motto: All or nothing.'[3]

For the moment it was nothing. The search for work continued, but half-heartedly. 'How does one attune the lyre', he asked Baille rhetorically, 'to the workman's tool or the clerk's pen?'[4] What little money he had soon ran out and Zola found himself reduced to borrowing small sums from the few friends left to him. He later recalled that at this period in his life he often had to make do with one meal a day, 'and that meal a pennyworth of bread and a pennyworth of cheese, or perhaps a few fried potatoes or some apples, or roast chestnuts bought at a street corner'.[5] When not actually looking for work he went off on solitary rambles in the outskirts of the city, along the banks of the sad little River Bièvre, or else spent the afternoon loitering by the open-air bookstalls on the quays, which constituted, he said, his 'free library'. Then he would return to the poky, unheated room he rented, wrap himself up in a blanket and continue writing fairy stories or sublimely ethereal verse.

10 The back streets of the Latin Quarter as they appeared when Zola was living there

He was continually on the move; evictions for failure to pay rent were the usual reason for a change of address, but he remained always on the left bank, never far from the Sorbonne and the Panthéon. His fortunes were at their lowest ebb in the winter of 1861–2, when he had a furnished room in a house in the Rue Soufflot; nowadays a very respectable street, leading into the Boulevard Saint-Michel opposite the Luxembourg Gardens, but at that time, when the Boulevard was still in process of being built, a slum area of the worst kind. Zola's room was in a sort of doss-house used by students, common prostitutes and pimps, 'a house where scandalous orgies alternated with free fights, and where the police made frequent, brutal raids'.[6] His memories of this semi-brothel served him later for certain passages in *Nana*, and it was also during this hard winter that Zola discovered the squalid sadness of the sex-life of the poor. It was a sombre, sordid, but educative episode. At the age of twenty-one, Zola was the same idealistic adolescent as he had been four years before, when he had been wordlessly worshipping the girl with the mop of ink-black hair under her pink bonnet. His head was full of impossible imaginings: of some pale-complexioned, fair-haired maiden of the north, wearing a crown of purple verbena on her head; of a brown-skinned country girl, moving through the long stalks of ripe corn and throwing him a warm smile as she passed; of the couches strewn with roses, the marble pools and perfumed fountains of an oriental harem. And he was living in an icy garret where the damp made the cheap paper peel off the walls. One evening there was a tap on his door: a snuffling old hag mumbled to him about a girl she was looking after who had been taken with some kind of a fit; could he keep an eye on her for a couple of hours ? The room he was taken to was as dingy as his own and more untidy, and the girl asleep on the truckle-bed—Berthe, the old woman called her—had a bloated face and seemed prematurely aged. Some dream, or the impatience of the fever, made her toss the blanket aside and Zola, mesmerized by the sight of the first woman's breasts he had ever seen, did not think to re-arrange the bed-clothes. A few minutes later she opened her eyes, and seeing the grave young man sitting there, stretched out her arms with a well-practised smile.

A few days later, having been evicted from her room, she knocked at his door. He had no wish to take her in, but she insisted: after all, he had had her for nothing. It was an argument that left him helpless; besides, he had a vague idea of enacting in reality the old romantic dream of the fallen woman redeemed through love. The first need was to teach her the dignity of labour; but Berthe proved an unwilling pupil, preferring to slouch around in sulky idleness. One evening he scraped together enough money to take her to one of the numerous working men's dance-halls. She sat beside him, toying with a glass, as morosely silent as ever, but he was astonished to find on their return that she had not missed anything and had enjoyed every moment.

As the winter set in, and his own attempts to find work continued as fruitless as before, he too fell into a hopeless lethargy. He stopped going out, and took to staying in bed all day with Berthe, for warmth's sake and for the poor comfort her body could give him. One evening, when neither of them had eaten for twenty-four hours, he told her to take his only pair of trousers, sell it, and buy some food. Already, one bitter night, as they were crossing the Place du Panthéon, he had taken off his coat, given it to her to pawn, and hurried back to the Rue Soufflot in his shirt-sleeves. Now he could not, for decency's sake, do anything but stay in his room. When a visitor dropped in, he pretended he was unwell. One of them— Pajot, or Villevielle—let it out that it was supposed he was living on the girl's immoral earnings. It may be that, in his indignation, Zola at last summoned up sufficient resolution to throw her out, or it may be that Berthe simply left him for a livelier and less penurious lover.

In January 1862 he wrote to Cézanne, alluding obliquely to this rather shameful adventure. 'I am very ill, but not dead yet. My mind is active

11 Zola, aged twenty, as painted by Cézanne (lithographic copy of a lost original)

and doing wonders. I even think that suffering is maturing me. I can see and hear better. I have acquired new senses that have been lacking in me for judging certain things. It seems to me that I shall be better able to depict certain aspects of life than I was a year ago. In a word, my horizons have widened and if, one day, I can write, my touch will be firmer, for I shall write out of personal experience.'[7] In the same letter he gave his old friend the good news that his long search for employment was at last over. At the end of the month he was to start in the publishing house of Hachette; only in the dispatch office, it is true, but how much better to work for a publisher than a draper or a druggist! It was a stroke of luck that he owed to the recommendation of another of his father's old friends, a professor of medicine called Boudet, to whom he had made application at the end of the previous year. At the time there was nothing Boudet could do but, distressed at seeing the son of the brilliant engineer he had known looking so shabby and famished, yet unwilling to hurt his pride by offering a tip, he had handed him a list of addresses and asked him to deliver his New Year cards. Some of these cards Zola found were to be left at the houses of former class-mates of his at the Lycée Saint-Louis. But he was never so glad as when, having done all the rounds, he called on Boudet again to receive the 20-franc gold piece that had been promised him in payment.

4 Cézanne and Gabrielle

Zola left his lodgings in the Rue Soufflot on the expiry of his year's lease and moved to a two-room apartment on the top floor of a converted nunnery in the Impasse Saint-Dominique (now the Impasse Royer-Collard). It was a pleasant house with wide staircases and high, narrow windows; Zola's attic room looked out over a garden planted with tall elms. The rent was reasonable: 20 francs a month, a fifth of the salary Hachette was paying him, but of course he had to work off all the small debts contracted during the eighteen months he had been unemployed and, besides, he wanted to do what he could to help his mother. Her father having in the interval died, she was alone in the world now and came to live under the same roof as her son, on the ground floor. The official registers denote her as an *ouvrière*, implying she was making a living by manual work of some kind, though whether as sempstress, charwoman or washerwoman is a matter for speculation. It is not impossible that, like the heroine of her son's masterpiece *L'Assommoir*, she worked for a while as a laundress. Some time before the end of 1862 the names of Mme Zola and her son appear in a list of tenants in a house overlooking the Montparnasse cemetery, the Rue de la Pépinière (now called the Rue Daguerre). A little way down the street there was a laundry of exactly the kind Zola was later to describe in the opening chapter of his novel.

This district was more purely working-class than any he had known before, and in due course his vivid memories of the Rue de la Pépinière were to colour the descriptions he wrote in *L'Assommoir* of the Rue de la Goutte-d'Or where Gervaise Lantier had her little shop and where, later, in a kennel-like room at the end of a corridor in a huge tenement house, she was to die of starvation. The building he and his mother lived in housed between two and three hundred persons, and hummed with activity from morning to night. The top floor was let out in single rooms to young workers, some of whom, like Zola himself, had a widowed mother to support. There was no shortage of jobs for such men: the economy was booming, and builders' labourers, stonemasons, roofers, glaziers were in great demand for the new houses and restaurants that were being rushed up to line the straight, broad boulevards of Haussmann's modernized Paris. Zola was astonished at the serious-minded industry of these young apprentices, who were taught their trade with blows and curses. It was a grim life they led, with few amusements: an occasional visit to the theatre to see some old-fashioned melodrama or one of the swashbuckling historical plays of Alexandre Dumas and, on Sundays, noisy parties in the taverns, the *guinguettes*, dotted around outside the city walls. The incessant hard physical labour was to drive most of them to drink before they were much older; very few, he noted, took advantage of the evening classes in the workers' institutes to try and 'better themselves'.

Clerks and shop assistants, the class to which Zola now belonged, had a long working week too: the office hours were from 8 a.m. to 6 p.m., with an hour and a half off for lunch, six days a week; sometimes, when a lot of business had accumulated, they would be kept at work till ten in the evening. These were not the best conditions for a budding author practising his craft in his spare time. Even so, he battled on, painfully adding page to page, working into the small hours and often on Sundays too. He had now given up poetry and was concentrating on the short stories later to be collected in his first published volume, the *Contes à Ninon*. It was in the Rue de la Pépinière that he wrote the finest and most intricate of them all, *Celle qui m'aime*, a story centring on one of the

12 Cézanne's impression of Zola reading one of his compositions aloud

fairground peep-shows that were so popular among Parisian working-class people.

In the autumn of 1863 Zola and his mother moved back to the 5th *arrondissement*, this time renting a three-room flat on the Rue des Feuillantines. It was here that he started holding the Thursday evening receptions for a small group of friends, which were to continue almost without interruption down to the outbreak of war in 1870. Originally the guests were all young men who had come up to Paris from Aix to pursue their studies or seek their fortunes: Marius Roux, Philippe Solari, Baille and Cézanne, together with a younger man befriended by Zola, Antony Valabrègue, the only one in the group, apart from the host himself, who had literary aspirations. At a later stage Cézanne took to bringing along one or more of his painter friends, Pissarro or Frédéric Bazille, and Zola would listen avidly to the discussions they embarked on.

Cézanne's first visit to Paris, in 1861, had been brief and unsatisfactory. Zola had been pressing him to come, and making plans for the good times they would have together when he did, but after the first few days he found his Paul unusually preoccupied and withdrawn. In any case, they saw disappointingly little of one another. Cézanne spent all his mornings at the Académie Suisse, the drawing-school where he first met Pissarro, and most of the rest of the day in the studio of another art student from Aix, Villevielle; so that except when Zola sat for the portrait he had suggested Cézanne should paint of him, they hardly ever met. This portrait caused Cézanne endless trouble; finally, in a fit of discouragement, he destroyed it. 'Paul may have the genius of a great painter,' Zola observed when reporting this incident to Baille, 'but he'll never have the genius to become one. The slightest obstacle puts him off.'[1] Not only did he lack persistence, but he would not listen to the calm voice of reason. 'Proving something to Cézanne is as hard as persuading the towers of Notre-Dame to dance a quadrille. He will pretend to agree, but won't budge an inch. . . . He won't even argue his point of view; argument bores him, in the first place because he finds talking tiring, and secondly because he would have to change his mind if his opponent proved to be right. . . . If he happens to put forward some view different from yours and you raise objections, he loses his temper before even considering the point you are making, shouts that you don't understand the first thing about the question, and branches off on to something else.'[2]

In September 1861, despondent at the slow progress he seemed to be making and, it may be, irritated at the new argumentativeness of his friend, Cézanne returned to Aix, determined to put his painting behind him and see if he could settle down to learn his father's banking business. But his demon went on tormenting him, and he was back in the capital in November 1862. By this time, of course, Zola was working long hours at Hachette's and it was he, rather than Cézanne, who had too little time to do justice to the claims of friendship.

13 Cabanel's *Birth of Venus*. A prime example of the kind of academic art against which Manet was reacting in the 1860s

Still, he could hardly avoid hearing from Cézanne about the rumpus that was brewing in the first few months of 1863 over the question of the spring art exhibition. Under the Second Empire the selection of canvases to be hung at this exhibition, the *Salon* as it was called, was the responsibility of a committee drawn chiefly from painters who had won honours in the past and teaching members of the Institute of Fine Arts. Being middle-aged men whose reputations had been made a long while ago, they tended to be conservative in their tastes; nevertheless they had usually made room, however grudgingly, for innovators, and at the 1861 *Salon*, which Zola had toured with Cézanne, they had accepted Manet's two submissions without too much argument; one of these pictures by the twenty-nine-year-old artist, a *Spanish Guitar-Player*, even achieved an 'honourable mention'. But in 1863 the jury seems to have decided that the time had come to rid French art of the impurities of modern 'realism'. The consequence was that, out of the 5,000 pictures submitted, no fewer than 3,000 were rejected, among them all the works sent in that year by Manet. When the news broke, there was an uproar in the artists' studios the like of which had never been witnessed before, and Napoleon III, after consulting with the Minister for Fine Arts, Nieuwerkerke, decided to authorize the holding of an alternative exhibition, a *Salon des Refusés* as the newspapers quickly named it; it would be held separately from the official exhibition, in a suite of rooms in the Palais de l'Industrie specially set aside for the purpose.

The authorities were gambling on a certainty. If the new wave of painters headed by Manet had few friends in the Institute, they had none at all among the public at large; a fact that was made painfully clear to Zola when, on the first Sunday he had free, he allowed himself to be piloted round the *Salon des Refusés* by a Cézanne bubbling with enthusiasm and speechless with rage at one and the same time. The crowd was enormous, since on Sundays there was no charge for admission, and the two friends had to listen to all kinds of outrageous comment, not only from wisecracking drapers' assistants but also from dignified representatives of the artistic establishment. It was above all Manet's principal exhibit, *Le Déjeuner sur l'herbe*, that provoked these sallies. Listed in the catalogue as *Le Bain*, the picture showed two young men, probably art students, sitting on the grass with the scattered contents of a picnic basket in front of them and a tree-lined river in the background. The third member of the seated group was a totally nude young woman, turning on the spectator a gaze of inscrutable immodesty. In all kinds of ways this composition violated the taboos of the period. There were plenty of

14 Manet's *Déjeuner sur l'herbe*. 'Zola was overwhelmingly moved by this picture'

studies of the female nude in the official *Salon*, but none showing a woman posing in such a matter-of-fact way alongside two men in modern dress. The 'realism' came out in the pallor of the flesh tints, natural enough in a mid-nineteenth-century girl not given to sunbathing, but contrasting strikingly with the improbable nacreous rosiness of the nymphs and goddesses painted in the approved pseudo-rococo style.

Zola was overwhelmingly moved by the picture. As yet he knew too little to be able to distinguish what was essentially revolutionary in Manet's masterpiece, but the subject itself made a profound appeal. We have already said something about the sensual pleasure he used to experience as a boy when he went bathing in the deep, tree-shaded waters of the Arc. *Le Déjeuner sur l'herbe* hinted at a link between these narcissistic delights and the more overtly sexual excitement suggested by the model's bare arms, powerful thighs and heavy breasts. But as he stared, an unwilling *voyeur*, at the big, uncompromising canvas, he was also aware of the hubbub around him, the sneers and the scoffing. 'Tell you what it is, the lady is too hot, while the gentleman has put on his corduroy jacket in case he catches cold.' 'No, she's blue already, the fellow's just fished her

15 Portrait of Alexandrine-Gabrielle Meley

out of a pond, and he's resting at a safe distance, holding his nose.' Zola moved away and watched the crowd from a corner, seeing, to quote the terms he later used when he transposed the scene in his novel *L'Œuvre*, 'the faces reddening in the warmth of the room, each with the round, stupid mouth of the ignoramus pronouncing judgement on art, all of them together uttering every idiotic remark, incongruous reflection, inane and malevolent guffaw that the sight of an original work can arouse in the vacant mind of the bourgeois.'[3]

There were other Sundays that summer when he and Cézanne would escape from Paris altogether, taking the first train of the day to the outlying village of Fontenay-aux-Roses, on the edge of the Forest of Verrières, not far from where Chateaubriand found a quiet refuge after he had fallen out with the first Emperor, the great Napoleon. Cézanne was loaded up with easel, paint-box, palette and brushes; Zola had a book stuffed into his pocket. From the wayside railway station they walked across meadows yellow with buttercups to a little inn kept by a friendly old soul known as la mère Sens. In her younger days she could remember the place being invaded by painters belonging to the new school of landscapists formed shortly before the 1848 Revolution; Courbet himself was alleged to have had a hand in painting the inn-sign, a tumbling still life of poultry, game, and vegetables. After breakfasting there, the two friends would push on to Aulnay, across fields of strawberries, and wander into the woods, making for their favourite spot, a certain pool covered with duckweed and edged with soft grass. Cézanne would set up his easel and paint industriously, while Zola lay on his back, his book forgotten in the grass beside him, blinking at the blue sky as it showed through the gaps in the bright green foliage.

Two years later, in the early spring of 1865, Zola revisited the Bois de Verrières, not this time in Cézanne's company but in that of a tall, striking brunette whom he called Gabrielle. When they were tired of looking for wild strawberries—it was rather too early in the year to find any—they would lie under the trees and talk about everything under the sun except, probably, art. Zola courted her shyly but passionately all through the following summer and autumn, but it was not until Christmas Eve, 1865 that she accepted him as her lover. Gabrielle—Alexandrine-Gabrielle Meley, to give her her proper name—was no Berthe. Neither was she an unripe adolescent, like Louise Solari; she was, in fact, a year older than Zola. According to one persistent legend, for which there is no proper corroborative evidence, Cézanne had enjoyed her favours before Zola, having first seen her posing in a life class. But the fact that Gabrielle had the physique to be a model is no proof that she ever was one, and there is the further point that Cézanne was notoriously timid where women were concerned. The clue may lie in the strange plot that Zola devised for one of his earlier novels, *Madeleine Férat*, which itself was an expanded narrative version of a three-act play, *Madeleine*, written in the very year

(1865) when he was courting Mlle Meley. The heroine loses her virginity to a medical student, who when he qualifies leaves her to take up a post abroad. Subsequently she meets another young man, who falls desperately in love with her. Apprehensive of the consequences were her first lover to return, she demurs a long time before yielding to his entreaties, though without telling him the real reason for her reluctance. In the novel, as in the earlier play, the first man does reappear, with various disastrous and melodramatic consequences, but we need not suppose that these are any more than fictional embroideries.

Her birth certificate shows that Gabrielle was the chance offspring of a temporary teenage liaison: her mother, Caroline Wadoux, was only seventeen at her birth, and her father, who gave her her surname, a year older; he is described on the birth certificate as a hatter. The two young people remained together, for a while at least, until Edmond-Jacques Meley wandered off and settled down with another woman whom he married. At that time the little girl he had fathered was nine. A year later her mother too was married; her marriage certificate shows that she was then working in a flower shop. The man she married, Louis-Charles Deschamps, was a riding-master, but her parents-in-law seem to have owned a florist's establishment in the 2nd *arrondissement*, and it was there, no doubt, that Caroline was working when she met her future husband. Tragically, she died only six months after being married, and it seems that it was the Deschamps who charitably took charge of the little love-child, Alexandrine-Gabrielle, their son's stepdaughter.

In later life, after she had become Mme Emile Zola, with a large house and a staff of servants, Alexandrine was, understandably enough, very unwilling to talk about her early life. Her husband loyally supported her in this policy of discreet reticence, with the result that all kinds of stories gained currency about her origins. Some said she had been a laundress, others that she had served behind the bar in some sleazy hotel. The probability is that Mme Deschamps taught her the business of a florist and that she followed this trade, at least in the beginning. Those who knew her well were impressed by her encyclopaedic knowledge, unusual in a town-bred woman, of the varieties of flowers and of the best ways to cultivate them; equally striking is the number of florists Zola introduces into his novels, notably in *Les Mystères de Marseille* and *Le Ventre de Paris*; in *L'Assommoir* there is a whole chapter given over to a circumstantial account of how flower girls were taught their job.

Though her adolescence may well have been spent in this sheltered environment, once she had grown up she began leading a more independent life and when Zola first knew her she was making her living as a sempstress. In those days, when women's dresses were never sold ready-made, there was plenty of call for cutters and needlewomen, and they formed a class by themselves; the younger, prettier ones were popularly called *grisettes*, after the sober grey gowns they habitually wore, though their reputation was not exactly that of chaste, nun-like creatures. But of course older women too plied the trade, and we can well imagine that Zola's mother took in such work when she had the chance. It is known that from 1862 onwards Mlle Meley had the tenancy of a modest apartment at No. 10, rue de Vaugirard, near the Odéon, and therefore not very far from where the Zolas were living. The circumstances of their trade would have been enough to bring the two women together, in which case it may well have been through his mother that Zola first met his future wife. This would account for the fact that, to judge from the few surviving letters from the widow to Emile and Gabrielle, written when the two young people were away on holiday together, her relations with her son's mistress seem to have been excellent.

Indeed, it could be said that Gabrielle took in the Zolas, instead of being accepted by them, for in July 1866, writing to his friend Numa Coste, Emile gave as their new address: 10, rue de Vaugirard. He and his mother had simply moved into the flat that the young woman had been renting for the past two years. It was quite commodious, with a parlour, a dining-room and kitchen, and, most conveniently, a spare bedroom.

5 The Publishing Business

Louis Hachette had started Zola at the bottom of the ladder, but the intelligence and initiative he displayed soon showed him to be fitted for a post of greater responsibility. The new employee had been in the firm for less than four months when he addressed a memorandum to his chief suggesting the launching of a magazine, to be called the *Bibliothèque des Débutants*, which would specialize in printing the work of young and promising writers who had yet to make their name. Although Hachette did not believe such a publication would pay its way, he was impressed by the care Zola had taken in working out the details of the plan; here was a man of ideas who deserved encouragement. Needing, as it happened, some reliable executive to look after sales promotion, he sent for him, told him his salary would be doubled and that from then on he would be in sole charge of that side of the business.

Zola's duties consisted mainly in composing advertisement copy for all the new books published by Hachette and persuading reviewers to give them favourable notices. The job brought him into personal contact with many of the firm's established authors, among them Duranty, who had proselytized for the realist movement in literature when it had been in its infancy, the popular novelist Edmond About, and Hippolyte Taine, the literary historian whose uncompromising materialism Zola was to embrace, a little later, with uncritical fervour. In addition, he found himself hobnobbing with the literary editors of the various newspapers and magazines of the capital and corresponding with others in the provinces.

All this experience of the practical side of the publishing trade was useful, and even necessary, for a would-be author. Zola found himself rapidly discarding any illusions he might have had about the part played by simple literary merit in the building of reputations. Writing to his young protégé in Aix, Antony Valabrègue, Zola promised to lend him a hand if he decided to come up to Paris to make his way. 'I can give you a few good tips; I'll be able to pass on to you what my experience has taught me, and we'll seize the bull by the horns. If you knew, my poor friend, how little talent counts in achieving success, you would abandon pen and paper and start studying the ways of the literary world, the innumerable little knaveries that force locked doors, the art of pulling strings and the ruthlessness necessary to step over the bodies of your dear

16 The dispatch office where Zola was first employed at Hachette

colleagues.'[1] Such cynicism is surprising, but in its essentials Zola's picture of the literary world was not greatly distorted; Balzac had drawn one not dissimilar in *Un Grand Homme de province à Paris*, though this was a book Zola had probably not read at the time. Authors and reviewers worked on the assumption that services rendered would be repaid, that a word in the right ear at the right time could work wonders, that one did not run down another man's book if there was a chance he would be reviewing yours—unless, indeed, you worded your attack in such a way as to give the book the kind of notoriety that would result in increased sales.

Zola's quickness in learning these lessons was demonstrated when his first book, the *Contes à Ninon*, was published in December 1864. Even the way he set about finding a publisher illustrates the practical acumen Zola was acquiring. In the spring of 1864 one of the periodicals Hachette owned, the *Revue de l'Instruction publique*, began reporting on a series of public lectures on cultural topics: the role of the crowd in Shakespeare and Aristophanes, Saint-Simon's memoirs, Balzac's views on the married state, etc. Zola had the job of writing these reports and although he allowed himself occasionally to criticize some of the lecturers quite harshly, it is noticeable that he has never anything but good to say about one of them, a certain Emile Deschanel. Deschanel may indeed have been an interesting lecturer, but he also happened to have considerable influence with the publisher Jules Hetzel. Not surprisingly, it was Hetzel who agreed to bring out the *Contes à Ninon*.

The young author knew better than to wait quietly for reviews to appear. He wrote his own 'blurb', sent it to all the newspaper editors he could count on for a friendly reaction, and even offered to save them the trouble of paying a reviewer: he would let them have a critical article on the *Contes à Ninon* written by 'a friend of his' which they could insert gratis. He also called on all the contacts he had so far made in the publishing world to help him push the volume, with the result that it was given an almost embarrassingly indulgent reception. Zola's only complaint was that far too many of these flattering critics had quite clearly not read the *Contes à Ninon* and had written about the book on hearsay, 'with the result that their readers must be judging me to be the most mawkish and saccharine creature alive. That's friendship for you! I would have rather had a proper hatchet job!'[2] He was beginning to learn that an author may sometimes be better served if he comes under attack than if he finds himself showered with indiscriminate praise.

The *Contes à Ninon* did, however, attract one honest review. It was signed by Jules Vallès, who was to make a name for himself a few years later as one of the leaders of the Paris Commune and as the author of a savagely satirical trilogy called *Jacques Vingtras*, written during his subsequent exile in England. Vallès's early struggles had been even more bitter than Zola's, but by the 1860s he had acquired a certain reputation as a hard-hitting journalist. The paper for which he worked wanted to send him to London, and in order to familiarize himself in advance with the English social scene Vallès decided to read through some of Dickens's novels, of which Hachette happened to have the French translation rights. Calling in at their offices, Vallès was directed up a spiral staircase and along a corridor lined on either side by stacks of unbound sheets; in a small office at the end of the corridor he was greeted by Hachette's *chef de publicité*, whom he remembered as a short man with an olive complexion, very black hair and what Vallès called a 'disdainful, almost supercilious mouth'. Their business was quickly transacted—to Vallès's gratified surprise Zola told him that, as a newspaper correspondent, he was entitled to the books free of charge. Then the two men started exchanging notes about past experiences and the hopes they entertained for the future. All of a sudden Zola raised his eyes and asked the other point-blank: 'Do you feel you are a power?' Vallès hardly knew what to say in answer to this blunt question but Zola, paying no attention, went on: 'Speaking for myself, I feel I am one',[3] and, without adding a word more, turned his mouth down into the same curiously disdainful curl. The remark was intended as a simple statement of fact.

Vallès, having duly received his review copy of the *Contes à Ninon*, pointed out perceptively the vague eighteenth-century perfume that clung to Zola's stories and mingled strangely with 'a sniff of contemporary realism which can be apprehended rather than actually detected'. But he continued on a warning note. 'The papers are full of his name and everywhere one reads nothing but complimentary epithets. But these adjectives smack of advertisement, and M. Zola ought to be wary of these ovations. Let him—as I imagine he can—silence all these sycophants who for the most part have not read his book, and let him rely for success solely on his energy and talent, of which he has enough not to need hired applauders and flatterers. He will be better off without them and criticism as a whole will benefit too.'[4]

These sage words may not have fallen entirely on deaf ears, but the feeling of insecurity that dogged Zola, a feeling attributable to the steady decline in his family's social and economic status ever since he was of an age to notice such things, needed desperately to be dispersed by the heady fumes of success. He had suffered too many rebuffs and failures in his youth not to want to take every possible precaution against their recurrence, especially now that he had embarked on the one career he counted on to bring him financial security and a measure of fame. He had to feel himself, in the words he used to Vallès, a *power*; it would not have been enough to be a middlingly successful writer.

So his second published work, *La Confession de Claude*, which was in the bookshops less than a twelvemonth after the *Contes à Ninon*, was the object of an even more carefully mounted publicity campaign. The blurb, which again he composed himself, called it 'a physiological and psychological study, a tale of blood and tears, with the pure, lofty morality of the fall from grace and subsequent redemption. . . . The author reveals himself as possessing a strange talent, made up of exquisite delicacy and frantic audacity . . .',[5] etc. Such hyperbole hardly accords with what Zola really felt about his maiden novel. Privately, he judged the book to be too sentimental in tone, too rhetorical in style. Having been started in 1862, directly after the collapse of his attempt to reclaim the prostitute Berthe, *La Confession de Claude*, which presents a flowery and over-dramatized account of this experiment, corresponded to a stage in his development that he had already outgrown, and he was almost annoyed with Valabrègue for praising it so highly. 'It still contains', he told him, 'much that is puerile. Here and there it flags, the observer retreats into the background and the poet reappears, a poet who has drunk too much milk and eaten too much sugar. The work is not virile, it is the cry of a rebellious, fretful child.' But he ended his letter to Valabrègue on a note of satisfaction. 'Today, I am known, feared, and insulted; today I am classified among the writers whose works are read in fear and trembling.'[6]

La Confession de Claude did cause something of a scandal when it appeared. There were passages the printer felt hesitant about, and understandably, for in those days the law regarded him as co-responsible with the author for any blasphemous or obscene text issuing from his press; the printer who had set *Madame Bovary* had been hauled before the magistrates along with Flaubert when the government decided to institute proceedings to have the novel suppressed. Improbable as it may seem today, there was some question of indicting Zola over *La Confession de Claude*. In the end nothing happened. The state prosecutor, asked to give his opinion, reported that the novel was unquestionably in bad taste. 'Obedient to the tendencies of the realist school, the author has on certain pages allowed himself too much licence in the analysis of shameful passions.'[7] But the final advice given was that, taking account of the moralistic intentions expressed in the book and its edifying conclusion, there was no case for prosecution.

The Public Prosecutor's report also contained the essential details about Zola's origins, schooling, career to date, present earnings, professional activities, etc. which, since he had no police record, could only have been elicited by inquiries made at his place of work. Now Hachette was a highly respectable firm, and the partners (old Louis Hachette had now died) were none too pleased that one of their employees should be achieving this particular kind of notoriety. Zola was not sacked; but it was pointed out to him that he might do better now to devote himself wholly to his career as a writer. His books were no very important source of income: the *Contes à Ninon* had not earned him a penny and the ten per cent royalty he received for *La Confession de Claude*, even after the whole of the first edition had been disposed of, would not have brought him in more than 750 francs. But he had been contributing regular articles for a year or two now to a couple of provincial newspapers, one at Lille and one at Lyons, and had been writing occasional copy for a popular Paris tabloid, *Le Petit Journal*. Then in November 1865 one of the most enterprising newspaper proprietors of the period, Henri de Villemessant, launched a new daily bearing a title made famous during the 1848 Revolution by Victor Hugo: *L'Evénement*. At Hachette's Zola had made the acquaintance of Villemessant's son-in-law and, after sounding him out, applied to join the staff of the new paper. What he had in mind to write was a kind of literary gossip column, in which he would talk not about books that had appeared but books that were about to appear; there would be indiscretions about the authors, background material about the books, advance extracts lifted from galley proofs. Zola felt confident that he had sufficient contacts among the writing and publishing fraternities to undertake to do this.

Villemessant, always on the look-out for novel ideas, was much taken by this one, and told Zola he could start in February 1866; he would pay him 500 francs a month. Thereupon, dazzled, Zola put in his notice at Hachette's for the end of January. The period of relatively secure, but relatively poorly paid salaried employment was over, and he was now fairly launched on the tumultuous but treacherous seas of journalism.

17 Painting by Cézanne showing his father reading *L'Evénement*, the newspaper for which Zola was writing in 1866

6 The Art Critic

When Zola had become rich and famous, with thickening body and thinning hair, he used to say that 1866 was the year he looked back on with the keenest nostalgia; it was, to use his word, *magnificent*. He was free, his time was his own: no more clocking in at the office. Thanks to Villemessant's munificence, he had at last enough to live on without worrying about the rent. 1866 was the year of his honeymoon with his first real mistress; and he spent his days in the company of friends of his age, some of whom wore leaky boots and patched coats, but all of whom seemed to be filled with the same superb self-confidence as he felt himself. They wrote their unpublished works in garrets, or painted eccentric pictures in ill-heated studios; but mostly, they strode the streets of Paris, which 'seemed to them too narrow to contain their ambitions. Each of us felt he had only to strike the pavement with his heel to cause such a masterpiece to spring into being as would dazzle the age.'[1] They would argue loudly with one another, wandering around in groups, until late at night; they stood gesticulating under street-lamps or sat round a café table, disdainfully indifferent to the passers-by who threw them timorous or indignant glances; until in sheer exhaustion, hoarse from shouting, their heads spinning with the extravagant theories they had been weaving, each would find his way back to his lodgings and stumble up the stairs to bed.

These young men were not, on the whole, those that had visited Zola in his office at Hachette's or those he had gone looking for in the editorial rooms of newspapers. He retained numerous contacts in the literary world, but his real friends, those with whom he spent his time in this kind of excited discussion, were almost all young painters and sculptors.

We have seen how frustrating had been Zola's efforts to get Cézanne to talk sensibly and rationally about his art. But Cézanne did render his old friend one valuable service: he put him in touch with those who could explain these mysteries in a way that Zola could follow. After they had visited the *Salon des Refusés* together, Cézanne took him round some of the studios where his fellow artists worked. In this way Zola met and became friendly with Camille Pissarro, one of Cézanne's oldest acquaintances in Paris (the two had met at the Académie Suisse during Cézanne's first, abortive stay in the capital), and with Frédéric Bazille, who had recently come up from Montpellier and was combining an apprenticeship to art with the study of medicine. Bazille was a pupil of Gleyre, an old-fashioned teacher who, however, was tolerated even by his most

18 Interior of the Café Guerbois, sketched by Manet

avant-garde students since he did not insist on their adhering to the strict formal rules of the Ecole des Beaux-Arts and charged them only nominal tuition fees. Among those who attended Gleyre's classes in the early 1860s were Monet and Renoir, both struggling along on limited means; Bazille knew them well and it is possible that he introduced Zola to them. But the man chiefly responsible for Zola's artistic education was none of these, but a certain Antoine Guillemet, a minor landscape painter specializing in views of Paris. He was a handsome man with an engaging manner and it was he who, in February 1866, first took Zola along to the Café Guerbois to 'meet the gang'.

The Café Guerbois, on the Avenue de Clichy in the Batignolles district of Paris, was patronized not just by artists but by critics too and others with a fringe interest in art, such as the celebrated photographer Nadar. It was traditionally on Friday evenings that the group, led by Duranty, got together round two tables reserved for them on the left of the street entrance to thrash out the articles of faith of the school that was already coming to be known as the 'Ecole des Batignolles'. At the time Zola started visiting the Café Guerbois, by no means all the leaders of the future Impressionist movement were to be seen there: certainly not Renoir or Sisley; Cézanne, Pissarro and Monet made only occasional appearances; Whistler never stayed long, Manet never came, and Degas's visits were widely spaced. The only 'regulars' were Guillemet, Bazille, and Fantin-Latour.

19 Manet seated before the easel in a painting by Fantin-Latour. Zola stands behind the chair with his right hand raised. The other standing figures include Renoir (wearing a hat) and Bazille (with his hands clasped behind his back)

However, the talk Zola heard there and, during daylight hours, at Bazille's studio which was another favoured stamping-ground, was enough to convince him that the approaching 1866 *Salon* would be likely to cause as much commotion as that of 1863. Manet's *Olympia*, exhibited the previous year, had provoked quite as much angry comment as his *Déjeuner sur l'herbe* at the *Salon des Refusés*. The question was, would the jury have the temerity to reject his submissions once more? Whatever happened, there was sure to be a storm, and Zola made up his mind to be in the thick of it.

His motives for intervening were mixed. He had a strongly developed streak of loyalty to his friends; it is true that at this time he had not yet met Manet, but Cézanne would be sending something in (his submissions were invariably rejected) and many of his newer artist friends would be doing the same. He had absorbed, with the rapidity natural to a born reporter, the essential ideas being bandied about at the Café Guerbois, and felt he could represent them in a challenging way if he were given the chance. The rebel in him looked forward to the opportunity of publicly cocking a snook at the authorities, meaning in this instance the bemedalled professors of the Ecole des Beaux-Arts. He was certainly attracted by the idea of winning notoriety in a new sphere: already known as the author of a maiden novel of brazenly uninhibited frankness, presently engaged in consolidating his reputation as a literary critic of advanced views who wielded a dangerous pen, he had the chance now to come to the fore as an equally iconoclastic art critic. Finally, and perhaps most importantly, he was genuinely moved by what he had seen of the work of the Batignolles painters. He appreciated their audacity, their readiness to break with tradition, and he believed they were inspired by the same creative aims as he was in the literary sphere. Whether painting woodland scenes or naked women, they were trying to show what they saw, and to get away from what Baudelaire had denounced as *le poncif*, stereotyped imitation; they were seekers after truth, enemies of cant; they did not see art as a device for mediating consoling myths, but as an instrument for the discovery of reality.

In those days there was hardly a newspaper in Paris that did not report on the annual art exhibition; these reviews, which also went under the name of *salons*, were moreover not confined to one issue, but frequently extended to a whole series of articles running for several weeks. It was certain that *L'Evénement* would follow the general custom and so Zola, before anyone else could stake a claim, went and saw Villemessant and asked to be given the job of writing the *salon*. The editor questioned him, saw that Zola had some interesting ideas and seemed to know what he was talking about, and gave his consent; the one proviso was that he should use a pseudonym. Zola decided to sign himself 'Claude', a deliberately transparent pen-name.

The opening day for the exhibition at the Palais de l'Industrie was always 1 May, but in order to put the cat among the pigeons before any of his fellow critics had had time to write a word, Zola published the first two articles of his *salon* at the end of April. He began on a supremely impertinent note: 'Before passing judgement on the artists admitted to exhibit, it seems only right that I should begin by passing judgement on the judges.'[2] Who were they, how were they chosen to exercise their functions, how conscientiously did they discharge them? Drawing on the stories he had heard his friends exchange, Zola named them one by one and gave his opinion in a few incisive and usually dismissive words. A few were artists of proved worth: Corot, Daubigny, Théodore Rousseau; but even Rousseau, who could not forget the long years he had had to spend in the wilderness, was too soured by past experiences to look with any indulgence on rising young hopefuls. As for the others, slick, fashionable painters like Cabanel and Meissonier, ageing relics of the romantic revolution like Isabey and Robert Fleury, assorted incompetents and nonentities like X and Y, they adjudicated, Zola maintained, according to their whims and prejudices or in fulfilment of this or that shabby bargain.

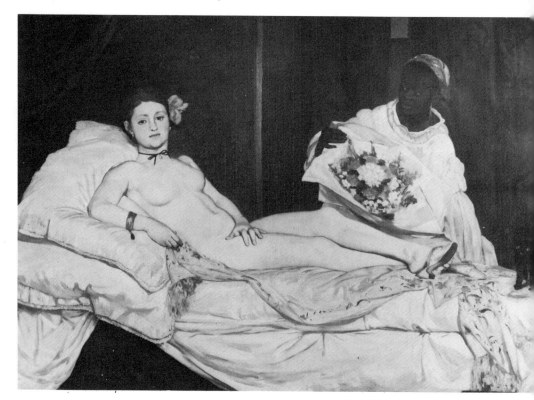

20, 21 *Olympia*, Manet's picture of a young prostitute lying on a sofa, and a contemporary humourist's impression of the work

In those days the law of libel was seldom evoked in France. The common procedure, when one found oneself traduced in print, was to issue a challenge and in this instance it was only his pseudonym that saved Zola from having to fight at least one duel. Villemessant was inundated with letters of protest, some of which he published, while others he declared to be unprintable by reason of the intemperate language in which they were couched. In a succeeding article Zola tendered his apologies to any individual members of the jury who might have been hurt by anything he had written. But of course he had already attained his objective: everyone was talking about his *salon*, the newsagents could not cope with the sudden extra demand for *L'Evénement*, and at the Café Guerbois that Friday Zola's drinks were on the house.

However, there was more to come, and the fat was well and truly in the fire when subscribers to *L'Evénement* opened their copy on 7 May to discover that 'Claude' had devoted the fourth article of his series to Edouard Manet. Now Manet was not even one of the exhibitors, having had both his submissions rejected though neither of them had been specially revolutionary. This affront was clearly a matter of pre-arranged policy: by excluding him, the establishment was making him pay for his impudence in sending in, the previous year, his picture of a young prostitute lying naked on a sofa, the picture he had called *Olympia*. In his article, Zola wrote appreciatively both of *Olympia* and of one of the rejected pictures, the charming *Fife-Player*; he declared Manet to be a master, predicting that in ten years' time his canvases would be selling for fifteen or twenty times their present price, and that the day would come when these masterpieces, so unjustly denigrated, would be hanging in the Louvre.

With this defiant panegyric of an artist whom nearly everyone at the time regarded as an irreverent jokester whose jokes were not even in very good taste, Zola found to his cost that he had overstepped the bounds. Public outrage was such that a number of readers of *L'Evénement* wrote in to cancel their subscriptions, and Villemessant, deciding the experiment had gone far enough, told his art critic to wind up the series. In the concluding two articles, Zola found space to salute in passing Monet's full-length portrait of Camille Doncieux: 'Monet—there's a man with individuality, there's a man, in short, in this flock of eunuchs. Look at the canvases either side, and see how pitiful they appear beside this window thrown open on nature!'[3] He expressed the gravest reservations about Courbet, whose recent concessions to the debased standards of public taste he found disappointing in the extreme. What had happened to the leader of the realist movement since those legendary days when he was producing such stark masterpieces as the *Burial at Ornans* and the *Bathing Women* of 1853? In comparison the *Woman with a Parrot*, his principal exhibit in 1866, was merely pretty. He wrote a few hasty words in praise of the three landscape painters he admired most: Corot (if only

22 Photograph of the upper reaches of the Seine, where he used to picnic as a young man, taken by Zola later on in life.

he would consent to dispense with those diaphanous nymphs improbably sporting in his forest glades), Daubigny, and above all Pissarro. Then he ended with a defiant declaration of his artistic principles:

> I have said: 'What I look for in a picture is the man, not the picture.' And again: 'Art is made up of two elements: nature, the fixed element, and man, the variable. For those who are true to nature, I give two cheers; I give three for those who are true to themselves' . . .
> I defended Manet, as I shall defend all my life every honest individuality under attack. I shall always be on the side of the vanquished. There is an obvious conflict between the unquenchable creative temperament and the crowd. I stand for the creative temperament and I attack the crowd.[4]

In spite of his disappointment at being cut short, Zola's mood when he signed off was optimistic, even euphoric. He had, after all, achieved everything he had set out to achieve, and more: a new notoriety among the public at large, an enhanced reputation as a polemicist, and the gratitude of the one painter he sincerely admired. Guillemet and Duranty had taken him along to Manet's studio and introduced him to the artist just after he started his *salon* in *L'Evénement*. Zola wrote his article on Manet with the memory fresh in his mind of the canvases he had been shown; and the day it appeared, Manet wrote him a charming letter of thanks. It was the start of a friendship that, with a few vicissitudes, was to last until Manet's death in 1883.

The rest of that summer was spent in well-earned relaxation. It had been years since Zola had been able to afford a holiday; but Cézanne had discovered a delightful retreat at Bennecourt, a riverside hamlet some six miles from Mantes, and in July Emile and Gabrielle joined him. Accommodation being short at the one and only inn, they put up at the local smithy; the only disadvantage was that they were awakened at first light by the swallows that nested on the chimney-top, and again at six by the ringing of the blacksmith's hammer on the anvil immediately beneath their room. By and by an assortment of friends flocked down to join them: Baille, Valabrègue, Philippe Solari and his girl-friend, and Antoine Guillemet. They spent the whole time on the river, rowing about in a bulky old boat lent by the innkeeper. There were islands on which to picnic, mysterious creeks to explore which wound away under dense foliage, quiet inlets where water-lilies floated. They set forth while the morning mists hung over the surface of the water like the milky breath of the river, and sometimes it was midnight before they returned, steering by the light of a full moon, with nothing to be heard but an owl hooting or a bullfrog croaking, while the waves danced and glinted in their wake. The hot streets of Paris, the angry passions and ugly rancour, the fears, aspirations and disappointments seemed very far away, trivial, almost meaningless.

7 Zola and Manet

The hazards of freelance journalism were brought home to Zola later that same year, when *L'Evénement* suddenly closed down. At that time the French press was still operating under the restrictive provisions of the decree of 17 February 1852, one of the effects of which was to draw a sharp distinction between journals that were permitted to discuss questions relating to 'politics or social economy' and those that were not. Permits for newspapers in the first category were granted sparingly, while the article prohibiting all discussion of political topics in newspapers of the second category was interpreted with the utmost strictness; in 1863, for instance, the editor of a local newspaper at Tarbes was held to be guilty of a contravention when he published an article dealing with the rebuilding of the town jail. No 'non-political' newspaper was allowed to make the slightest reference to any administrative act whatsoever initiated by the state, and it was because Villemessant printed a comment which could be construed as reflecting on the policing of the theatres in the capital that *L'Evénement* was suppressed on 15 November 1866.

For Villemessant this was no more than a setback. He owned another newspaper, *Le Figaro*, which had been running for twelve years as a gossip rag appearing twice a week. The reason for this odd periodicity is to be looked for in another provision of the press laws under the Second Empire. To ensure payment of any fines the courts might impose, each newspaper proprietor had to deposit caution-money with the Treasury, but a lesser amount was required for journals appearing fewer than three times a week. Obliged to cease production of *L'Evénement*, Villemessant paid the additional deposit necessary to turn *Le Figaro* into a daily newspaper. This ensured that there was no drop in his revenues but, of course, with only one paper to run he no longer needed the staff he had engaged for two. He found room for a few of Zola's pieces in *Le Figaro* at the end of 1866 and in the first couple of months of 1867, but refused to employ him as a regular contributor.

New Year's Day 1867 also saw the last of Zola's contributions to *Le Salut public*, a Lyons paper to which he had been sending sizeable literary essays every fortnight for the past two years. Deprived of both his sources of income, he found himself once more reduced to expedients of the most pitiful kind. Gabrielle addressed parcels for Hachette and badgered the cashiers of little magazines that owed Emile money but were themselves on the verge of insolvency. He stayed at home, scribbling away at a monstrous penny-a-liner called *Les Mystères de Marseille*, a piece of work he would never have undertaken had he not been at his wit's end for a little ready cash. His old school-friend Marius Roux, knowing his difficulties, had put him in touch with the editor of a Marseilles paper called *Le Messager de Provence*. This man, Alfred Arnaud, had the idea of increasing the paper's circulation by publishing in it a serial story based on various notorious court cases that had captured local interest within living memory. Roux ferreted out the details, and Zola based the rambling plot of his novel on the law reports and press cuttings his friend sent him. Like Eugène Sue's *Mystères de Paris*, which obviously suggested the title, *Les Mystères de Marseille* was full of action and brisk dialogue; its concluding chapters describe the stirring events of 1848 as they affected Marseilles. Zola wrote it solely for the 200 francs a month it brought him; but, although he freely admitted that its literary value was negligible, he never repudiated it, arguing that any honest work a man does to keep body and soul together cannot be called disgraceful.

The sudden dip in Zola's fortunes was made all the harder to bear by the circumstance that Paris, that year, was crammed with visitors from the provinces and abroad who had, it seemed, money to burn. Throughout most of the Second Empire it had been a city 'éprise du plaisir jusqu' à

23 The huge building on the Champ-de-Mars specially erected for the 1867 Exhibition

l'atrocité', in Baudelaire's words: 'pursuing pleasure to the point of pain'; but in 1867, the year of the Great Exhibition, gaiety reached a new peak of frenzy. A quarter of a century later, Zola synthesized his memories of that summer in a bitterly satirical passage of his novel *L'Argent*:

It was on April 1st that the World Fair of 1867 opened, marked by celebrations of triumphal splendour. The great season of the Empire was beginning, that supreme gala season which was to turn Paris into a hostelry catering for the entire world, a hostelry all decked up, with music and singing and fornication in every bedroom. There had never been a reign which at its zenith had bidden all the nations to so colossal a bean-feast. As in the grand finale of a pantomime, the long procession of kings, emperors and princes wound its way from the four corners of the earth towards the Tuileries Palace blazing with lights.[1]

The actual Exhibition, housed in a huge, oval-shaped brick building specially erected on the Champ-de-Mars, was for most foreign visitors no more than a convenient pretext for being in Paris, that 'sovereign city, abode of pleasure' as Meilhac and Halévy called it in the libretto they wrote for Offenbach's operetta *La Vie parisienne*. The operetta, with its catchy tunes, daring costumes, and frivolously inconsequential plots, was the art form that best typified all that was most heartless and perverse in the age. For Zola, it was inevitably associated with this period of hectic merry-making, and whenever he had occasion thereafter to mention Offenbach, the musician who 'conducted the can-can of the 1867 World Fair',[2] he could never conceal his scorn and irritation.

The exhibition at the Champ de Mars was devoted not just to the newest products of technology; it included a picture gallery for a large retrospective display of contemporary French art. Manet, realizing there was little chance any of his work would be hung, paid for a temporary showroom to be built in the Place de l'Alma. He had disappointingly few visitors; even Courbet refused to go, protesting he could not understand Manet's painting and would only be disagreeable to him if he met him there. 'It's hardly been a great financial success so far', Zola told Valabrègue. 'The thing's not been properly launched. I hope my pamphlet will set fire to the powder keg.'[3] The pamphlet in question, published as a 'biographical and critical study' of Edouard Manet, may not have made many converts but did at least help to keep the artist in the public eye. What few references it attracted in the press were ironically dismissive: Zola was compared to Abu-Bekr, Mohammed's father-in-law, threatening to put to the sword anyone refusing to recognize the Prophet. Manet himself was touched by the staunchness of his young defender, and offered to do the art work for an illustrated edition of the *Contes à Ninon* if a publisher could be found willing to take the risk. Nothing came of this project and so, instead, Manet decided to execute Zola's portrait and make him a present of it.

This was not the first time Zola had posed for his portrait. We have

24 Manet's portrait of Zola, exhibited at the 1868 *Salon*

already seen how, in 1861, he succeeded in persuading Cézanne to paint him though not, in the event, to finish the work. Zola sat for him on other occasions, but the only portrait by Cézanne, antedating Manet's, of which we can be certain that Zola was the model, is a painting now lost, and known to us only through a lithographic copy, which shows the writer with bent head, the light striking his broad, high brow while the jaw-line and beard remain in deep shadow.

Manet did not start on his portrait of Zola until November 1867. The sittings, which took place in the painter's studio in the Rue Guyot, were something of an ordeal: Zola found that if he changed his position in the slightest, Manet would throw down his brush and refuse to continue. He posed seven or eight times in the studio and then early in 1868 Manet, anxious to complete the picture in time for the *Salon*, visited the apartment Zola was renting in the Rue Moncey in order to fix the background details. The background, in Manet's mind, assumed immense importance; he was aiming at something far more significant than the conventional 'author's study' setting. On the canvas the rather cluttered wall immediately behind the sitter shows a copy of the famous *Olympia* underneath a reproduction of a Velazquez painting (Velazquez was Manet's favourite Spanish artist), which has a Japanese print set alongside it; like Whistler and Degas, Manet was fascinated by the specimens of Japanese art that dealers were then shipping over to Europe in quantity. All this gives the impression of an almost suffocating invasion of the model by the artist. In the half-dozen pamphlets arranged fan-wise behind the porcelain inkpot, only one can be confidently identified by the title, and that is Zola's 'biographical and critical study' of Manet: the name on the cover is prominent enough to constitute a signature for the picture. It is significant that Zola is not shown at work. He sits bolt upright, his legs idly crossed, holding in his left hand an open book that he is not even reading; his eyes are fixed elsewhere, or perhaps nowhere.

It is difficult to think of any portrait in the history of art that tells us less about the subject and more about the artist who painted him. Not that this idea ever crossed Zola's mind. Having early adopted the motto that all publicity is good publicity, he could not have been other than delighted when the portrait was accepted for exhibition at the 1868 *Salon* and consequently seen by thousands. The critics were kinder to it than they had been to any of Manet's previous works; Gautier praised it and so too did Castagnary, who singled it out as one of the best portraits in the whole exhibition, though he was perceptive enough to observe that the accessories had been given rather more loving care than the human subject.

It is tempting to imagine that the reflective, almost visionary look in Zola's eyes, which Manet captured so well, corresponded to something in his mood at the precise moment when the portrait was painted. For this was a time for stock-taking and long-term decisions for Zola. He had plans, certainly, to build on the reputation he had already won in the fields of literary and art criticism: he wanted to write a study of Courbet, and on the fly-leaf of one of his publications he had announced as forthcoming a book with the suggestive title *L'Œuvre d'art devant la critique*. These were projects never, in the event, carried out; instinctively, Zola knew that his real future lay in creative rather than critical activity.

This intuition was confirmed when he finished writing *Thérèse Raquin*, the first of his novels about which he had no private reservations. He had started it in the new year, and by the beginning of April 1867 had completed the first part; his mornings were devoted to this work, of which he had such high hopes, and his afternoons to the less exacting task of turning out instalments of *Les Mystères de Marseille*. The greater part of *Thérèse Raquin* was written in the summer of 1867; it was published in November, just about the time when Zola started sitting for Manet.

Thérèse Raquin is the first work of Zola's that has stood the test of time and makes as compulsive reading today as it did when it first appeared. Even before he had finished it, he told his confidant Valabrègue that it would be 'assuredly my finest work. I believe I have put myself into it

25 The covered way in which Zola situated the haberdashery shop where Thérèse
Raquin lived with her husband and mother-in-law

body and soul.'[4] This remark ('je crois m'y être mis cœur et chair') invites
us to see it as a subjective creation, a personal confession like his maiden
novel. But this is clearly not what Zola can have meant. None of the
characters can be identified with him and the story that gave him his plot
was lifted directly from a crude thriller by a third-rate novelist, Adolphe
Belot, with whom he was personally acquainted. Belot's novel, itself
founded on a real-life *cause célèbre*, tells how an adulterous couple
conspire to murder the woman's husband, are exposed, brought to justice
and executed. The most important among several variations that Zola
introduced was to eliminate the discovery of the murderers' guilt. Thérèse
and her lover Laurent bring off the 'perfect crime', one that is not only
never detected but never even suspected. They persuade Thérèse's husband, Camille, to go out with them on a rowing expedition; in a quiet

part of the river, unwitnessed, Laurent capsizes the boat, drowns Camille and then swims ashore with Thérèse.

This change enabled Zola to devote the second part of his book to the detailed and excruciating account of the nervous breakdown suffered first by Thérèse and then by Laurent; worn out by mutual recrimination and fear of betrayal, they both end by drinking a deadly draught from the same cup of poison. So obvious an application of the principle of poetic justice might seem tame; but in fact, the peculiar insight Zola possessed into the mechanism of the human psyche raises this banal scenario on to an altogether higher level of intuitive analysis. Thérèse has been driven into Laurent's arms by the most nakedly primitive of sexual urges: left unsatisfied and unfulfilled by Camille's languid love-making, she finds herself excited beyond all thought of resistance by the powerful odour of robust virility exuded by the large-limbed, thick-necked peasant's son whom her husband brings home one fatal evening. Laurent in his turn is roused by the frantic eagerness of her response. What neither of them realizes is that the murder they decide on, although of course it achieves its original objective of freeing them to indulge their passion undisturbed, in fact destroys it by killing their desire for one another. This was the startling truth that Zola stumbled on: that the link between love and death, or more precisely between the act of killing and the act of sex, is so close that having committed the first, neither Thérèse nor Laurent can find any further satisfaction in performing the second. They marry, of course—why go to the lengths of murder if it is not going to bring you its rewards?—but only to discover that the old fervour has leaked away. At first indifferent to one another, they soon reach the point where living together is a torture; afraid to separate, they are forced to play the public comedy of the happy couple until despair and disgust finally drive them to sunder, in the only possible way, the bonds of horror and guilt that tie them inextricably to each other.

In order to achieve his effects, Zola had to make his two central characters moral idiots. No sense of pity, decency, or compunction could be allowed to deflect them from the course their instincts impel them to follow. In the preface he wrote for the second (1868) edition of *Thérèse Raquin*, Zola implicitly recognized this when he stated that Thérèse and Laurent were characters 'without souls'. They were, he said, human animals or beasts in human form; the term he used, *des bêtes humaines*, was to provide him many years later with the title for one of the darkest and most blood-stained novels in the *Rougon-Macquart* series. He also alluded obliquely in this preface to one of the most ostensibly hostile reviews the book had received, the writer of which referred to *Thérèse Raquin* as a 'puddle of mud and blood', adding for good measure that Zola 'sees woman as M. Manet paints her, muddy in colouring with pink make-up'.[5]

The denunciation had been fierce enough to arouse public curiosity, which was, in fact, the intention of both reviewer and author. The first edition of *Thérèse Raquin* had been selling slowly; Lacroix, the publisher, found he was barely covering his costs. Zola thereupon had a word with Louis Ulbach, who had financial interests in Lacroix's business and was also literary editor of *Le Figaro*. The general line followed by Ulbach in his review may well have been suggested by Zola in order to provide the cue for his lengthy rebuttal, which was published in the same newspaper a few days later and undoubtedly helped to arouse new interest in his novel.

Whether connivance was as close as this or not, the fact is that the parallel Ulbach drew between Zola and Manet was not one that Zola himself could take offence at; on the contrary. There is also more aptness in it than Ulbach's review by itself would suggest. One of the most striking aspects of the women's faces in both *Le Déjeuner sur l'herbe* and *Olympia*, the two canvases by Manet that had caused the greatest furore when they were exhibited, was precisely what could be called their 'lack of soul'. Manet painted his models as pure objects: neither their mouths nor their eyes betray what they are thinking or indeed whether they are thinking anything at all. Their naked faces are simple prolongations of their naked bodies; in pictorial terms they are the very same *bêtes humaines* that Zola claimed to have depicted in *Thérèse Raquin*. Yet it would be wrong to regard this as a case of a painter influencing a writer; rather, the two men's minds and imaginations happened to be running on parallel tracks. This accounts for the insight and sympathy with which each was able to interpret the personality of the other, Zola in his monograph on Manet, and Manet in his portrait of Zola.

8 Beginnings and Endings

The letter to Valabrègue already referred to, in which Zola claimed to have put himself into his new novel 'body and soul', ends with a significant postcript: 'By the way, have you read the whole of Balzac? What a man! I am re-reading him just now. He towers over everyone else in this century. Victor Hugo and the others—for me at least—fade into the background. I am thinking of writing a book on Balzac, a full-scale study, a kind of novel based on reality.'[1]

This book was never written, though if one were to bring together all the various articles Zola published on Balzac between 1868 and 1880 there would be ample matter for one. Having resumed his functions as literary critic, Zola did his best to communicate his enthusiasm to his readers in reviews of successive volumes of the new edition of *La Comédie humaine*, which Michel Lévy was bringing out over these years. The result was that, at a time when Balzac's reputation was still far from firmly established, Zola very soon came to be regarded as his principal apologist after Taine. Critics discovered traces of Balzac's influence in his novels; his post-war publisher, Charpentier, used to introduce him to his friends with the words: 'Come and meet the new Balzac'; and the celebrated cartoon by André Gill, in which Zola is shown solemnly saluting a bust of Balzac who returns him his salute ironically, testifies to the popular view of the literary affiliation between the two novelists.

When one creative writer conceives so passionate an admiration for another, it is natural enough that he should try and analyse the nature of his predecessor's genius in order to repeat and if possible transcend his achievement. What struck Zola most in Balzac was the vastness and variety of *La Comédie humaine*, the sheer enormity of the fictional world he had created.

It is a dizzy pile of palaces and hovels, one of those cyclopean monuments such as one sees in dreams, full of splendid halls and shameful dens, criss-crossed by broad avenues and by narrow shafts along which one has to crawl on hands and knees; the storeys rise one on top of the other, some lofty, some cramped, in different styles; sometimes you find yourself in a particular room without any idea how you climbed up there or how you will get down again; you press on, losing your way a score of times, confronted always with new splendours and new horrors. Is it a brothel? Is it a temple? Impossible to say. It is a world, a man-made world, superb and shabby, put up by a prodigious builder who was also, in his moments, an artist.[2]

26 A cartoonist's comment on the literary affiliations between Zola and Balzac

This passage occurs at the beginning of an essay on Balzac published in *Le Rappel*, a newspaper founded by Victor Hugo's two sons and a group of his closest friends to prepare the way for the great poet's return from exile. The article on Balzac was the last of Zola's contributions accepted for publication in its columns, the editorial board having taken the view that it was hardly proper for such fulsome praise to be lavished on any other writer than the author of *Les Misérables*. One has the impression, however, as one reads the essay, that Zola may have been thinking only partly of *La Comédie humaine* when he wrote it; in his mind's eye he had a vision of his own massive work, *Les Rougon-Macquart*, which at the time he was writing (his article appeared in *Le Rappel* on 13 May 1870) had advanced well beyond the stage of being a mere project. The various component volumes had been sketched out and the first, *La Fortune des Rougon*, already written. Secretly, Zola felt convinced that when *Les Rougon-Macquart* was finally completed in five or ten years' time, it would loom as large in critical opinion as Balzac's *Comédie humaine*.

The idea of writing a connected series of novels first came to him in the autumn of 1868. At that time his material situation was causing him much less anxiety than it had a twelvemonth earlier. At the beginning of the year he had got himself on to the staff of a new left-wing paper, *Le Globe*, along with Jules Vallès; a dangerous colleague, Vallès, for it was an article of his, judged subversive, that led to the suppression of the newspaper only four weeks after the first issue. Fortunately Zola was able to move almost immediately on to another daily, *L'Evénement illustré*, for which he wrote copy of all kinds—sketches, stories, and even a *salon*, which was markedly less truculent than the *salon* he had written for Villemessant's now defunct *Evénement* two years previously. But it was above all the enactment on 11 May 1868 of the long-awaited new press law that transformed his personal prospects. This liberalizing measure, which did away with the need to obtain prior authorization before starting up a newspaper, resulted in a notable increase in the number of journals circulating in Paris. Employment opportunities for freelances like Zola improved correspondingly: whereas in 1867 he had succeeded in having only seventeen pieces published in the press, in 1868 he placed over a hundred.

With the return of financial security, he could allow himself to indulge in dreams of a long-term creative project. As he pondered the example of Balzac, it occurred to him that he would need to find some device to link together the various novels that would constitute *his* 'comédie humaine'. Balzac had solved the problem by inventing the 'reappearing character': Rastignac, Bianchon, Delphine de Nucingen, first introduced to the reader in *Le Père Goriot*, all turn up again in a dozen or more stories, where they meet and get involved with other characters who in turn reappear in other stories. The whole effect was that of an enormously complicated circuit diagram, in which the tangled lines representing the wiring stand for the links between the numerous reappearing characters, though of course such an image could not have presented itself to Zola any more than it could have done to Balzac.

Clearly it was out of the question for Zola to adopt the same device to give unity to his own projected novel-series: the imitation would have been too flagrant. So he hit on a slightly different idea: each of his novels would be concerned with some critical passage in the life of a particular member of the same family. It would need to be a family with wide ramifications, studied in different generations, but the hero or heroine of each of the constituent books would be related by blood to the hero or heroine of every other book. There would be brothers and sisters, aunts, uncles, nieces and nephews, offspring legitimate and illegitimate, distant cousins, so that the whole series would constitute the history of a family.

The particular slant this would give to the cycle as a whole accorded admirably with another aspect of the work, which in Zola's eyes was of paramount importance: its scientific character. He had not, at this stage, reached the point of elevating science to the status of a dogmatic religion, but he had some time ago acquired the conviction that scientific methods of exploring reality and discovering truth were destined in the near future

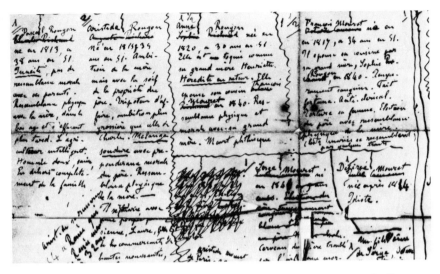

27 Section of the heavily corrected original draft of the Rougon-Macquart family tree

to displace metaphysical speculation or explanations based on scriptural revelation. Much that was at present mysterious would be clarified as science continued its steady encroachment on the domain of the unknown. Among the questions that Zola expected science to try and answer were those associated with human heredity: what caused this child to 'take after' one parent rather than another, how did it come about that siblings were sometimes so dissimilar, or that an inherited trait could skip one or two generations? The thirty-odd members of the Rougon-Macquart family would give him ample opportunity to illustrate every one of these familiar but inexplicable puzzles; and although of course he could not hope, as an ignorant layman, to offer authoritative solutions to any of the problems his books raised, at least he would be drawing the attention of better qualified men to their existence, and inviting them to apply scientific methods to their investigation.

But the real master-stroke lay in deciding to give the work that particular dimension which prompted Havelock Ellis to call it, when it was all completed, a 'study in social mathematics'.[3] Zola wanted his fictional family to typify what he called 'the vast democratic upheaval of our time'. The Rougon-Macquarts were to have their roots in the peasantry and were to be shown forcing their way upwards until their most energetic or fortunate members obtained a foothold among the upper echelons of society. 'The work will constitute in this way a study of the contemporary *bourgeoisie*. . . . I shall accomplish for the Second Empire, more methodically, what Balzac accomplished in respect of the reign of Louis-Philippe.'[4]

These remarks occur in the draft of a submission he prepared for his publisher Lacroix, whose backing it was essential he should obtain if he was to embark on the undertaking with confidence. Zola wanted Lacroix to agree to publish a total of ten novels, which he reckoned to write at the rate of two a year, so that the whole series would be complete within five years. Over this period he would need, of course, to support himself, his mother, and Alexandrine too if she stayed with him. He had talked about this problem with the Goncourt brothers, on the first occasion the two celebrated novelists invited him to lunch, on 14 December 1868. What he told them he needed was an assured income of 6,000 francs a year; the brothers, who were men of substantial private means and had no need to trouble themselves about what they earned from their writing, listened in politely ironical silence to these sordid calculations. In the end he got what he wanted: Lacroix consented to the arrangement, provided Zola agreed to make over to him the sums he expected to receive from the newspapers in which the books would be serialized in advance of publication.

By the spring of 1870 everything seemed to be set fair. Not only did Zola have his contract with Lacroix, but he had completed the first volume of the series, which described the origins of the Rougon-Macquart family in the small southern town of Plassans—for reasons of delicacy Zola preferred not to give it its true name, Aix. This book, entitled *La Fortune des Rougon*, had been accepted for serialization in *Le Siècle*, which in itself was a signal honour, since this newspaper enjoyed a wider circulation than any other in France at the time. Feeling sure of the future, or feeling it was time, at least, to put his affairs in proper order, Zola decided to end the irregular situation he was living in with Alexandrine-Gabrielle Meley. He married her in a registry office on 31 May, twelve days after learning from his old friend Philippe Solari that Louise, Philippe's sister, had died in Aix at the age of twenty-three. With her died one of the last of Zola's romantic illusions, embalmed in the very depths of his heart; embalmed but, as we have seen already, still potent enough to give life to the fictional creation of Miette Chantegreil, the teenage heroine of *La Fortune des Rougon*. Miette dies, tragically, killed by a counter-insurgent's bullet, and so too, a little later in the book, does her young lover, the idealistic Silvère who may be thought to incarnate the adolescent, romantic Zola now finally and irrevocably interred.

The year 1870 was one of endings and fresh beginnings not just for Zola personally but for the nation at large. On 19 July war was declared on Prussia; the long expected trial of strength was beginning. It quickly appeared that the Second Empire had in fact signed its own death-warrant. A series of lost battles in the first week of August compelled the French forces to evacuate the eastern province of Alsace. MacMahon's subsequent attempt to link up with Bazaine at Metz led to complete disaster: at Sedan, encircled and powerless, a whole French army capitulated and Napoleon III, sick and beaten, surrendered to the Prussians. This did not mean the end of the war but it did mean the end of the

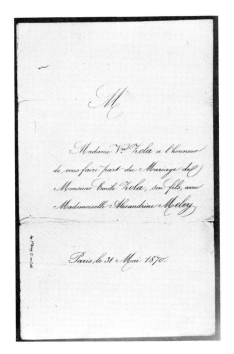

28 The card sent to their friends by Zola's mother to announce her son's marriage.
Note the dropping of the bride's plebeian first name Gabrielle

Empire. In Paris, on 4 September, a new Republic was proclaimed and the conduct of affairs put in the hands of a Government of National Defence.

In the days immediately preceding the outbreak of war, the mood in the country as a whole had been bellicose, not to say jingoistic. When the so-called Ems telegram was published—a statement to the press by Bismarck so worded as to appear a deliberate rebuff to the French—all the papers in the country except those on the far left took up the cry: 'March on Berlin!' Zola was one of the few to make a public stand against this wave of hysteria. Ever since he had started taking an interest in political matters, he had been critical of the warlike adventures that marked the reign of Napoleon III, and had not hesitated to express these misgivings in print. In 1868, for example, in the course of an article describing a visit to one of the cemeteries of Paris on All Souls' Day, Zola reported a conversation he had had with a poor widow who had no grave to mourn by and had asked him if he could tell her in which direction Sevastopol lay. Her three sons had all been conscripted into the army: one had died in the Crimea, another was killed in Italy, the third never returned from Mexico. The article is written as a plea to remember those of the dead who do not lie at rest in some French cemetery, but in 'some corner of a foreign field'; but the underlying pacifist sentiment is unmistakable.

After the outbreak of war Zola continued to publish articles in this vein in the republican paper, *La Cloche,* for which he was writing at the time, at the risk of being arrested for defeatism. In fact, the seditious tone of one of them, entitled 'Vive la France!', was such that the authorities could not overlook it, and Zola received a summons to answer a charge of attempting to discredit the government. News of the French defeat at Wissembourg came through, however, before he could be brought to trial, so that Zola never served the prison sentence he had courted. On the other hand he very soon found himself out of a job, for on 18 August *La Cloche* suspended publication. A letter he wrote four days later to Edmond de Goncourt—whose brother Jules had died of syphilis earlier that summer—shows the state of mind he was in at the time: 'This frightful war has made the pen fall from my hand. I am like a lost soul. I wander aimlessly around the streets.'[5] Then, on 7 September, he wrote again to the same correspondent to tell him he had made arrangements to leave for the south. Alexandrine was anxious about the way things were going and, besides, there was nothing to keep him in Paris. Down at Marseilles, on the other hand, he had some useful contacts: Alfred Arnaud, the editor of the *Messager de Provence* in which his *Mystères de Marseille* had been published, and the Barlatiers who owned the *Sémaphore de Marseille,* the most influential newspaper in the region; the head of the family, Emile Barlatier, had been a close friend of his father.

Arnaud suggested there might be room for a cheap paper—newspapers always sold best at times of crisis—and Zola got in touch immediately with his old friend Marius Roux, asking him if he would be interested in helping to edit a new daily to be called *La Marseillaise.* The venture proved, however, less viable financially than Zola had hoped, and before long he was looking round for some more lucrative form of activity, preferably in government service.

Zola had never exerted himself to cultivate politicians, but there was one senior republican statesman whom he felt he could approach with some confidence: this was Alexandre Glais-Bizoin, a veteran of the 1848 Revolution and one of the founders of *La Tribune,* an opposition newspaper which Zola had supplied with copious copy before moving over to *La Cloche* in January 1870. At the age of seventy, Glais-Bizoin found himself in Tours, sent there as a delegate of the Government of National Defence to organize local resistance. The letter Zola addressed him from Marseilles was a little devious and lacking in candour. He made no reference to the brief existence and approaching demise of *La Marseillaise.* He pretended to have been summoned to Aix by a group of well-wishers who wanted him to represent the city in the Constituent Assembly but, 'the elections having been postponed *sine die,* I have no wish to remain idle any longer. Has the Republic a post to entrust to me—a prefecture or a sub-prefecture? I would prefer not to leave the south, where I am very well known and where my father performed great services.'[6]

That Zola, with no previous experience, should have thought himself capable of holding important executive office in the provinces may seem surprising. But the recent history of the country suggested that once the new regime had established itself, many of those who had served the previous government would lose their jobs, and that the vacancies would be filled by men who had given earlier proof—as Zola had—of a firm commitment to republican ideas. There were precedents for writers occupying salaried government posts: the fact that Stendhal held consular office under Louis-Philippe had not prevented him from writing *La Chartreuse de Parme* during one of his furloughs. In the turmoil of war and invasion, was it realistic even to think of pursuing a literary career ? 'I imagined', he later said, referring to this period, 'that the world was coming to an end, that no more books would ever be written.'[7] In any case, whatever the future held, currently it seemed out of the question to earn a living in the way he had in the past; he needed to try a different tack.

His letter to Glais-Bizoin remained unanswered, which was hardly surprising, for the deteriorating military situation at the end of 1870 compelled the government to evacuate Tours and establish itself provisionally further south—at Bordeaux. Rather than write again, Zola set off on his own to make the difficult cross-country journey in a wartime winter. The snow was thick on the ground between Sète and Montauban, and it rained steadily thereafter. He arrived at Bordeaux to find the city swarming with refugees and hotel rooms at a premium.

He had come with the fixed idea of securing a nomination to Aix, confident that the pre-war holder of the post would not be allowed to retain it. But the government offices teemed with people like him hunting for jobs and he began to lose hope. 'At the present moment,' he wrote to Alexandrine, 'if I were to apply for a situation as gamekeeper I doubt if I would get it.' There were a few consolations: he found the Arcachon oysters succulent; but the weather continued as wet as ever and the trustiest friend he had was his umbrella. His purse was too light for a long stay, and in any case, 'every so often I get a surge of pride, thinking how superior I am to all these people. What a sorry thing it is I do, holding a begging-bowl out to the Republic! But just wait for them all to be swept away; then you'll see I'll find my feet again.'[8]

He was on the point of cutting his losses and returning to Marseilles, had in fact already secured his travel warrant, when he thought he should, as a matter of courtesy, pay Glais-Bizoin a visit. On his first arrival at Bordeaux, none of his friends knew where the old man could be contacted, and besides, they warned him that his patron was senile and had no real influence. However, when he finally ran him to earth, Glais-Bizoin received him so affably that Zola decided to defer his departure. Two days later, the minister offered to take him on as private secretary until such time as a suitable posting came through. Zola accepted with little enthusiasm; but at least the modest salary attached to the secretaryship would save him and his family from actual starvation. They joined him—his wife, his mother, and Bertrand the labrador dog—on 26 December, after a nightmare journey, the train having been blocked in the snow for twenty-four hours. Desperately short of money though they were and setting up house in a strange town with the weather now freezing cold, they could even so count themselves luckier than the friends they had left in Paris, besieged, bombarded, reduced to killing and eating cats and rats and cutting down the trees along all the avenues to burn as firewood.

Glais-Bizoin was as good as his word. He pulled what strings he could to get Zola appointed to a sub-prefecture at Bayonne, and it was no fault of his that another applicant was preferred. A separate attempt to secure him a similar post at Castelsarrasin also came to nothing, but then, at last, his luck turned. News reached him that, with the signing of the armistice, *La Cloche* would be resuming publication in Paris under the editorship of Louis Ulbach, the old friend who had written so providentially damning a review of *Thérèse Raquin*. Since the National Assembly was in session at Bordeaux, Zola was able to offer his services as parliamentary correspondent. Between 13 February and 12 March 1871, he sent daily accounts of the occasionally stormy proceedings, concerned principally with the preparation, discussion, and eventual ratification of the peace treaty. Once it was signed, the Assembly resolved to remove to Versailles and so Zola was able at last to return to Paris, delighted and relieved to find that his apartment, requisitioned in his absence, was in good shape and that all his papers were safe. Was it too much to hope that life would now return to normal?

9 From the Commune to *L'Assommoir*

If Zola thought to pick up the threads straight away, he was soon disillusioned, for it was only four days after his return that the people of Paris raised the banner of revolt and broke with the government led by Thiers which remained based on Versailles. The insurrectionary movement gathered strength rapidly: on 26 March 1871 a separate administration was set up, under the name of the Commune, which after by-elections rendered necessary by the resignation of the moderates, took on a distinctly revolutionary complexion.

During the first few weeks of the rule of the Commune Zola was able to continue his work as parliamentary reporter, leaving for Versailles every morning from the Gare St Lazare on the 'journalists' train' and returning to write up his account of the day's proceedings in time for the morning edition of *La Cloche*. There was an occasion towards the end of March when he got himself arrested at Versailles; luckily he was able to give the name of the son of the Minister of Education who had got to know him in the offices of *La Cloche* and could vouch for him. In fact, at no point did Zola express either open or covert sympathy with the long-term aims of the Commune and so long as the armed truce lasted between the Versailles forces and the insurgents inside the city he continued to hope that some compromise bargain would be struck.

However, as the days went by the situation deteriorated fast. On 6 April he took the precaution of leaving off his signature at the end of his articles; then, on 18 April, *La Cloche*, judged insufficiently revolutionary by the Commune, was suppressed. Zola had, however, another outlet for his journalism: about the same time as he started reporting on parliamentary debates for *La Cloche*, he had made an agreement with Emile Barlatier in Marseilles to send him similar bulletins and these continued to be printed in *Le Sémaphore* even after *La Cloche* had been closed down. The wonder is that he managed to get his dispatches delivered, considering the chaotic state of postal communications in France just then, but they all appear to have reached their destination and, in their totality, constitute a vivid account of the steadily worsening conditions inside Paris: the growing threats to freedom of speech and movement, the persecution of the clergy and the terror caused by the armed bands that patrolled the streets. But, unlike Edmond de Goncourt who was observing the same scenes and describing them venomously in his diary, Zola felt no hostility towards the working-class supporters of the Commune, only towards their leaders, the revolutionary activists whose one idea,

29 Fighting in the rue de Rivoli during the Paris Commune of 1871

he said, was to knock on the head everyone who did not agree with them.

In early May, reacting to the arrests of Communards by the Versailles authorities, the newly formed Committee of Public Safety began rounding up hostages inside the city. As a journalist known to have adopted a lukewarm attitude towards the Commune, Zola had every reason to fear arrest, and began to cast around for ways and means of getting out. The trains were still running; women and children and the old were allowed to leave without hindrance, and so too, curiously, was anyone who could produce a pass issued by the Prussian army authorities encamped on the east of Paris. Somehow Zola succeeded in procuring one of these and on 10 May he and Alexandrine took the train from the Gare du Nord to Saint-Denis, just outside the city limits, where a transit camp had been set up for refugees. A little later his mother was able to join them here, and all three went down to Gloton, a small village on the other side of the river from Bennecourt, to await developments. The crisis was not long in coming. On 21 May the Versailles troops forced their way into Paris; the savage street fights and burning of public buildings went on for a week, until the Communards were all either dead or taken prisoner. Zola re-entered the city before the bloodbath was properly over and sent an eye-witness account to *Le Sémaphore* of the horrific destruction wrought by both attackers and defenders. More characteristically, he described the stench arising from the unburied corpses that littered the pavements.

Gone were the rich aroma of truffles and the delicate scent of rose-water that everyone associated with Paris under the Second Empire. 'You enter it now holding your nose, as if penetrating into some foul-smelling sewer where rotting flesh is bubbling under a leaden sun.'[1]

The two-month rule of the Commune and its final, merciless suppression were events that left an indelible mark on French public life. Class warfare, which had been smouldering since the early 1830s, had at last burst into literal flame, and though the ensuing bourgeois backlash succeeded temporarily in cowing the working class, the establishment continued to be haunted by a neurotic dread of some future renewal of proletarian violence. Zola shared some of these fears, but he had lived too near the working classes, from whom both his wife and his mother originally sprang, to see them as the destructive barbarian horde that privileged aristocrats like Edmond de Goncourt judged them to be. When their leaders were put on trial in August 1871, Zola argued in the press that far from being the unprincipled ruffians the conservatives declared them to be, they were for the most part well-intentioned men misled by their own propaganda; and he had the courage to express his 'lively sympathy' for Courbet, that 'stupid fool of a great painter'[2] accused of having organized, among other outrages, the demolition of the Colonne Vendôme. On the other hand he never betrayed the least sympathy for the Communards' social and political programme. Even the few modest steps they took, when in power, towards humanizing industrial conditions—such as to forbid night work in bakeries—were ridiculed by Zola, who could see no justification for state interference in relations between masters and men. But once the rising was crushed and the Communards rounded up, he argued doggedly in favour of clemency and a rapid amnesty. These men were, after all, no criminals; and he was inclined to regard the whole episode as no more than an outbreak of collective insanity, explainable and excusable in the light of the terrible privations the Parisians had suffered during the preceding winter of siege and starvation.

The next few years were difficult ones for Zola. In the bleak economic climate of the early 1870s the book trade suffered as bad a slump as any since the early 1830s, and Lacroix was one of the publishers to go to the wall. It will be recalled that his contract with Zola allowed him to recoup the advances he was making to the novelist out of the payments forthcoming from newspaper editors for serialization rights on the *Rougon-Macquart* novels. The arrangement might have worked well if times had been normal; but although, as we have seen, the first book in the series, *La Fortune des Rougon*, was accepted for instalment publication in *Le Siècle*, there was a long delay before it actually started to appear. War broke out before all the instalments had been printed, and thereafter *Le Siècle* needed all its space for news from the front; so readers of *La Fortune des Rougon* were left in the air. In the meantime Zola had started work on the second volume of the series, *La Curée*, and by the time he moved from Paris

30 In this cartoon, drawn in 1875, Zola is seated on copies of the first few titles in the *Rougon-Macquart* series, examining through a lens Eugène Rougon, the hero of the sixth volume

down to Marseilles in September 1870 had written about three-quarters of it. The troubled life he led over the next eight months prevented him from finishing it until after the collapse of the Commune, and it was not until 29 September 1871 that the first instalment of *La Curée* appeared, this time in *La Cloche*. But it was as though a curse had been laid on the *Rougon-Macquart* series. On 6 November the author was invited to present himself at the office of the Public Prosecutor. This official had, it appeared, received a number of complaints about the immorality of *La Curée*, which would force him to take action against *La Cloche* unless Zola voluntarily discontinued its publication. He had no option but to yield to this veiled threat, though he did write an indignant letter, printed in *La Cloche*, in which he protested in the strongest terms against the narrow-minded prudery of the reading public.

By this time the unfortunate Lacroix had gone to smash. All these delays and interruptions meant that the revenue he had been counting on from the newspapers flowed in at a much slower rate than anticipated, while at the same time he was obliged by his contract to continue what were in effect a series of advances due month by month to the author. In return, Zola signed him promissory notes which, when Lacroix's affairs were being wound up, were discovered by his creditors, who then called on Zola to redeem them. This, of course, was something he was in no position to do, so a lawsuit was started and at one point a bailiff appeared on his doorstep with a warrant for his arrest. It was the kind of situation that Balzac, who was notorious for ruining his publishers, had found himself in more than once, but the parallel, if it occurred to him, could have given Zola scant comfort.

Quite as disturbing as the discovery that he was now up to his neck in debt was the realization that *Les Rougon-Macquart*, which were to bring him fame if not fortune, now risked foundering at the outset for lack of a publisher. The third volume, *Le Ventre de Paris*, was already mapped out, but although he knocked on a number of doors Zola could find nobody prepared to commit resources to a long-term project when the outlook for publishing generally was so dismal. Then one afternoon, as he was leaving the press gallery of the Chamber of Deputies, he was accosted by a total stranger with an invitation to call the following day on Charpentier, who wanted to talk business with him. Zola was more than a little staggered, for the house of Charpentier, though it had good standing, was reputed to be highly conservative in its publishing policy; it was one of the last firms he would have thought of approaching. However, the enigma was to some extent resolved when he presented himself at the publisher's office and found that the business was now being run not by old Gervais Charpentier who had founded it but by his son Georges, whose ideas were more adventurous. Zola put forward his proposal in the tone of a man mournfully convinced before he started that he would get nowhere. Essentially, he wanted a continuation of the same arrangement as he had had with Lacroix: the payment of a fixed monthly sum of 500 francs, in return for which he undertook to write two novels a year over the next six years; these works to become Charpentier's absolute property for a period of ten years. Zola concluded by warning his listeners that they should not count on making much profit on serial publication. After the way his last novel had to be withdrawn in the middle of the fourth chapter, newspaper editors would not be falling over themselves to sign him up.

Charpentier waived the point, and came back to the nub of the proposal. 'You're offering me twelve novels at 3,000 francs apiece, in other words I'm being asked to tie up 36,000 francs. You'll allow me twenty-four hours to think it over.'[3] Zola took up his hat and left; after the door closed behind him, Charpentier turned to his associate, Maurice Dreyfous, the man who had gone to the Chamber in search of their author, and asked him what he thought. It was agreed they should seek the opinion of Théophile Gautier, who was acting as their unofficial literary adviser; and Gautier, who had never met Zola, though of course he had read his books, urged Charpentier to close with the offer. 'He's not yet in control of his style,' the old poet remarked; 'it's convoluted, all tangled up, but he's a master of his craft.'[4]

A contract was accordingly drawn up along the lines that Zola had requested. Charpentier bought back the rights on Zola's earlier works from Lacroix, and was able to issue the next three volumes in the series, *Le Ventre de Paris*, *La Conquête de Plassans*, and *La Faute de l'abbé Mouret*, between 1873 and 1875. Of course, Zola had grossly under-estimated the time it would take to write them; instead of two novels a year it was proving difficult enough to produce even one, and newspaper editors were showing themselves quite as shy of bidding for serial rights as he had guessed they would be. Afraid he might be getting into the same difficulty with his new publisher as he had with his former one, that is, receiving more in the form of advances than his books were earning in sales, he broached the question with Charpentier. But it appeared that the *Rougon-Macquart* series was doing a lot better than he supposed. Charpentier got his accountant to work out what the novelist would have received if the contract had stipulated normal royalty payments of 40 centimes a copy, and it was discovered that on this reckoning Zola had been underpaid to the tune of 10,000 francs. Very handsomely, Charpentier offered to pay him this sum immediately, annul the original contract, and put him on a royalty basis for the future.

This windfall enabled Zola to settle all his old debts with Lacroix and, in addition, to take a summer holiday—the first since the war: he and Alexandrine spent the months of August and September at Saint-Aubin, a little fishing village on the Normandy coast. Zola, who knew only the tideless Mediterranean, could not get over his astonishment at the endless variety of the seascapes he saw from the cliffs of the Channel. None of the *Rougon-Macquart* novels had been planned to have a coastal setting, but he took copious descriptive notes none the less of stormy seas, calm, sunny seas, the phosphorescent foam of the breakers under moonlight, grey days when the ocean seemed to stretch to infinity, and filed them away against the day when he could make use of them in one of his books. In any case the original plan had already been modified and expanded; was there any reason why the *Rougon-Macquart* series, originally en-visaged as a group of ten novels, should not run to twice the number? Charpentier seemed to be in no hurry to see the saga finish. His relations with his publisher continued as cordial as ever and in the summer of the following year (1876) he and Alexandrine joined the Charpentiers at Piriac, on the Bay of Biscay, 'a charming spot', he told Alexis, 'at the world's end, with water all around us'.[5]

The healthy sales of the first half-dozen novels in the series had been achieved in spite of a notable paucity of reviews which Zola privately attributed to a deliberate conspiracy of silence. There may indeed have been some concerted movement on the part of the powerful coterie of Catholic-conservative critics to treat him with studied disdain, though

Barbey d'Aurevilly could usually be relied on to salute each new volume with a few colourfully denunciatory lines. The growing number of his friends and admirers were aware of this cold-shouldering and some of them, like the irascible Flaubert, were furious about it. 'Into what abyss of idiocy are we to sink?' he asked George Sand. 'Belot's last book has sold 8,000 copies in a fortnight as against Zola's 1,700 in six weeks for *La Conquête de Plassans,* and he hasn't had a single article.'[6] In fact, *La Conquête de Plassans* went down rather better than some of its predecessors in the series. Ferdinand Brunetière, a critic listened to with rapt attention in right-wing circles, went so far as to acknowledge that in scattered passages of the novel one could sense the touch of a real master; both he and Anatole France were impressed by the vivid character sketches of the quarrelsome, scandal-mongering burghers of Plassans. Criticism today tends to pass over *La Conquête de Plassans* in favour of *La Curée, Le Ventre de Paris,* and *La Faute de l'abbé Mouret,* which were given a bad press, or else largely ignored, when they first appeared. The reason for this critical shift is not hard to discover. *La Conquête de Plassans* was a *roman de mœurs* of a type made familiar by Balzac, Champfleury, and other less gifted novelists, whereas *Le Ventre de Paris,* with its hallucinatory evocation of the provision markets of the capital, and *La Faute de l'abbé Mouret,* with its dreamlike depiction of the vast luxuriant wilderness of Le Paradou—a vision by the Douanier Rousseau translated into words before any of the Douanier Rousseau's paintings were seen—these works were so startlingly original that the most contemporary critics could do was to blink and pass on to something easier.

There were, besides, ideological reasons for the mute hostility that greeted these novels. In the first few years of the Third Republic, no one could be sure that parliamentary democracy would not shortly be overthrown and replaced by an autocratic regime, of the kind Zola pilloried with such bitterness in *La Curée,* in *Le Ventre de Paris,* and in *Son Excellence Eugène Rougon,* the sixth novel of the series. Even though Bonapartism seemed spent as a political force, the possibility of a restoration of the monarchy was a very real one; and in any case, the post-war elections had returned an overwhelmingly right-wing Chamber of Deputies. It was a period of extreme political and religious reaction; almost, it might be said, the Empire still, but without the Emperor. So it was considered at the very least tactless of Zola to be constantly harping on the opportunism, graft, and police oppression that had stained the annals of the Second Empire. Why insist on raking up these old scandals? The real danger had surely been amply demonstrated during the Commune. Profiteers, place-seekers, political manipulators could be tolerated; but not another take-over of the state by industrial workers.

This was why *L'Assommoir,* which described in such vivid and convincing detail the conditions that had made the Commune possible and perhaps even inevitable, caused a thrill of horror to run through the same reading public that regarded the revelations in his earlier novels with impatient indifference. Properly to appreciate the impact of *L'Assommoir* one has to understand how the urban proletariat was looked on by the majority of the nation, whether members of the middle classes living in the towns or landowners and small farmers living in the country: with a mixture of repulsion, condescension, and suppressed dread. They were, of course, the necessary hewers of wood and drawers of water; as necessary as the thousands of horses that pulled carts and carriages through the streets; but not much more highly regarded. If they did their work satisfactorily, they were paid enough to keep them alive; if they grew too old or too careless to be worth their keep, they were not exactly sent to the knacker's yard—they were suffered to starve to death.

This attitude was so widespread that it was not necessary to be particularly callous to subscribe to it; and there is no doubt that Zola shared it up to a point, but only up to a point. Although born into a bourgeois family and given the usual education that the sons of middle-class parents received, he had found himself in his early twenties living cheek by jowl with the labourers and artisans of the Paris working classes. From personal observation he knew all about the risks they ran of accidents at work, the exhaustion and monotony of the long day's labour from which so many of them were driven to seek relief in bouts of heavy drinking, the almost total lack of recreational facilities, the coarseness of their sex-life, the brutality with which a few of them treated their children, the grimness of their latter end, with no provision for when they grew too old to work and no hope of anything but the uncertain charity of philanthropic institutions.

Zola showed all this in *L'Assommoir* with the graphic intensity that derives from intimate, first-hand knowledge; but he also showed how these people accepted their lot with a sort of dumb resignation and inability to imagine that it could ever be different. Since the action of the novel was supposed to take place in the early years of the Second Empire, there could be no question of any reference to the Commune; and in fact the only character in the book who interests himself in political questions, Auguste Lantier, is the least attractive of them all, a kind of spiv, an idler and a parasite. The absence of any overt political orientation in the book was one reason why it was so angrily denounced on the left; but this purely negative feature was not sufficient to commend it to the conservatives, who judged that the details Zola furnished of the disgraceful conditions in which men and women of the artisan class were condemned to live could only provide ammunition for the socialists regrouping themselves in exile after the terrible mauling they had received in 1871.

Thus, ironically, both left and right concurred in damning Zola for having misrepresented the working classes in *L'Assommoir*. His reply was that he had done nothing of the sort: the picture he had painted was completely truthful. His argument, implicit in the text of the novel but

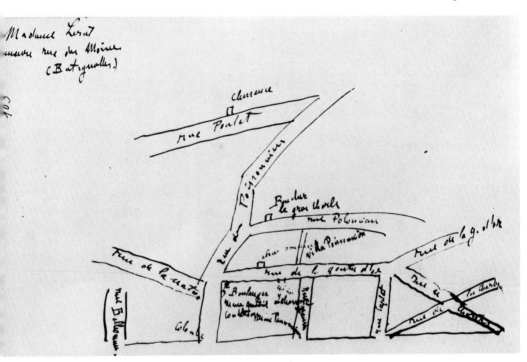

31 Sketch-map by Zola to show the location of the various shops mentioned in
L'Assommoir. At the bottom, the word 'Colombe' indicates the position of the gin-palace
nicknamed 'l'assommoir' by the locals

made explicit in a preface, was that it was up to the ruling classes to mend
matters by providing better housing for the labouring poor and better
education for their children, and by legislating against excessively long
hours of work for an inadequate wage. The evils he showed—promiscuity,
delinquency, alcoholism—were, he insisted, the inevitable results of a bad
environment, which only needed to be changed for the evils to disappear.
If changes were not made, there would be more workers' riots, more
disruption and violence; but in that case the middle-class leaders would
have only themselves to blame.

It is true that the phenomenal interest the novel aroused was due only
in a minor degree to such considerations as these. Mostly, it was the
revelation—upsetting but indisputably fascinating—that Zola gave of the
way of life of this class of people that made the book an immediate best
seller. The scene of the fight in the wash-house in the opening chapter set
the tone: two women, after a quarrel, start throwing buckets of water at
one another until, exasperated, one of them flings herself on the other and
tries to strangle her. It ends with the victor beating her assailant over the
bare buttocks with one of the wooden paddles used for dislodging the dirt
from wet linen. Later scenes were even more ugly, but they were not all of
this kind; some were infused with innocent gaiety and others with

32 Renoir's illustration of an episode in *L'Assommoir*. Nana, as a teenager, walking along the street arm in arm with her friends

heart-rending pathos; while the language in which Zola had chosen to write the greater part of the novel—the actual language, full of crude metaphors, used by the slum dwellers themselves—constituted another innovation which many regarded as an unforgivable lapse of taste. However, then as now, few readers were put off a novel by hearing it hotly denounced everywhere as a book that ought never to have been allowed into print. With the appearance of *L'Assommoir*, Zola was transformed overnight from being an author with a reputation for producing well-written but rather dull books concerned with the iniquities of the pre-war regime, into one who could compose a moving, dramatic, and horrifying story of contemporary life in one of its least known aspects. He had at last achieved his break-through and was now a public figure, perhaps more reviled than admired, but undoubtedly a power in the land.

10 Friends and Disciples

'A singularly friendless man'[1] is how Mrs Belloc Lowndes, who became acquainted with Zola when she was a young lady reporter working in Paris, described him in the memoirs she wrote some fifty years later. Zola himself, on more than one occasion, contrasted the marvellous comradeship said to have existed among the young Romantics in the 1820s with the mutual suspicion with which men of letters in his own time regarded one another. 'There is not a single *salon* in Paris where writers in their thirties can feel at home. The solitude is absolute. Every man fights under his own banner.'[2]

The complaint occurs in a newspaper article written in 1872, when Zola was perhaps feeling lonelier than he had since the black winter of 1861–2. Whether or not literature is served by the existence of literary coteries, it is a fact that throughout most of the nineteenth century, and not only during the Romantic period, there was a tendency for poets, and to a lesser extent novelists, to form small circles or *cénacles* meeting usually at the house of the leading member of the 'school'; and Zola yearned to find himself heading such a group. Though too introverted to be called sociable in the usual sense of the word, he enjoyed acting host to a select circle of friends, and we have already seen how before the war he had established a tradition of regular Thursday evening parties held in whatever modest apartment he was renting at the time; but we have also noted that his guests were almost exclusively artists and that most of them came from Aix. Such contacts as Zola had with the literary world of Paris were more formal and on the whole confined to the exchange of professional services.

Just before the war, however, he succeeded in striking up a personal acquaintance with the brothers Goncourt, two writers for whose work he had a genuine admiration. Having noticed how consistently this unknown journalist, writing in rather obscure newspapers, was praising each of their books as it appeared, Jules, the younger brother, finally wrote inviting him to lunch. Their impressions of him on this occasion, carefully consigned to their diary, provide a very characteristic but also penetrating portrait of the twenty-eight-year-old writer. What struck them chiefly was his ambiguous, almost hermaphroditic personal appearance: at once burly and frail, he looked more youthful than he was, 'with the delicate moulding of fine porcelain in his features, in the arch of his eyebrows'. Rather like the weak-willed, easily dominated heroes of some of his early novels, he seemed an amalgam of male and female traits, with the latter dominant,

33 The Goncourt brothers photographed by Nadar

the 'morbid, sickly, ultra-nervous side of him'[3] as the Goncourts called it.

There were other meetings, both before and after the death of Jules de Goncourt; but, in view of Edmond's age and more especially of his altogether higher social station, Zola never dared return this hospitality; in any case the fastidious middle-aged bachelor was a little stiff and unnerving.

Flaubert, on the other hand, that voluble, bawdy old Viking, was a man much easier to take to one's heart, for all the difference in age of nearly twenty years that separated him from Zola. The two men may not actually have met until after the war, although Zola ventured to send him a complimentary copy of *Madeleine Férat* on its publication. It was probably the enthusiastic review he wrote of *L'Education sentimentale* that brought him to the older novelist's attention, for this work had been honoured with so few notices when it appeared in 1869 that it seemed to argue special qualities of discernment to have singled it out for such warm and intelligent appraisal. At that time Flaubert, whose home was at Croisset, had a *pied-à-terre* in Paris in the Rue Murillo where on Sunday afternoons between three and six o'clock he entertained a small circle of writers which included Edmond de Goncourt and Alphonse Daudet.

Over the ten years or so during which Flaubert and Zola were in direct personal contact, each conserved a profound respect for the literary talent and achievements of the other. At the same time, they disagreed radically over certain questions occasionally bandied to and fro in their group. Zola was disconcerted when the 'Master' embarked on one of his frequent diatribes against what he regarded as the more tiresome features of the modern age: railways, newspapers, election campaigns. But Flaubert was equally puzzled when Zola risked some optimistic prophecy about the fuller life people would lead in the twentieth century thanks to scientific and social progress: 'he would look at me fixedly with his big blue eyes and then shrug his shoulders'.[4]

Another regular Sunday afternoon visitor in the Rue Murillo was the Russian novelist Ivan Turgenev, who belonged to the same generation as Flaubert and Edmond de Goncourt, all three men being at this time in their fifties. Although Zola knew and appreciated those of Turgenev's works that were available in French, he came to look on him more in the light of an obliging business connection than as a man of letters. Curiously, in the early 1870s, when he was still starved of recognition in his own country, Zola had already acquired a devoted following in the Russian Empire. He learned from Turgenev that extensive extracts from *La Fortune des Rougon* and *La Curée* had been quoted in two long articles in a St Petersburg literary magazine of liberal tendencies, while as early as 1872 a certain P. D. Boborykin, writing in another periodical on 'New Methods in French Fiction', had proclaimed him a greater master than either Balzac or Flaubert. The third of the *Rougon-Macquart* novels, *Le Ventre de Paris*, was published in two separate Russian translations, while with the fourth (*La Conquête de Plassans*) Zola was outselling all other French authors except the irresistible Jules Verne.

All this was encouraging news, but still it was mortifying to think that while he was struggling to make ends meet in Paris, publishers, hack translators, and editors of literary periodicals in Moscow were waxing fat on the fruit of his labours. There was no copyright convention in existence between France and Russia; but Turgenev, who in May 1874 was preparing to make a return visit to his native land, said he would see what could be done to channel some part of the flow of roubles into Zola's pockets. While at St Petersburg he saw M. M. Stassyulevitch, the editor of the influential monthly magazine *The European Herald*, whom he finally persuaded to accept an arrangement whereby Zola should post him galley proofs of his next novel sufficiently in advance of its scheduled instalment publication in Paris for the Russian translation to appear more or less simultaneously; in that way Stassyulevitch could count on being the first to publish Zola's new work in Russia, and he agreed to pay him a handsome fee for the privilege.

But there was even better to come. In January 1875, now back in Paris, and having spoken to Zola again at one of Flaubert's Sunday afternoon gatherings, Turgenev wrote to Stassyulevitch suggesting he should treat with Zola for a regular monthly article of substantial length on the 'literary, artistic, and social scene in Paris'.[5] This was the start of the long series of 'Letters from Paris' that Zola contributed to the *European Herald* over the next five years. The subject of each essay was chosen after consultation with Turgenev; Stassyulevitch himself would sometimes make suggestions, for instance that a study of Stendhal would not come amiss in the series; and occasionally Zola would send in a short story, a form of fictional writing he had neglected since the early days of the *Contes à Ninon* and to which he might well never have returned had it not been for the need to provide regular monthly copy for the *European Herald*.

In 1876 Stassyulevitch came to Paris and was able to make personal contact with his illustrious collaborator. All Zola told Turgenev about this meeting was that they dined together, and that he found Stassyulevitch 'charming' and full of ideas about future projects. Stassyulevitch himself, in a letter to a Russian friend, gave a rather more circumstantial account of the occasion. Zola had not been at home when he called, and when the door was opened he found himself confronted by a dog 'as big as I am who practically devoured me on the spot'. But Mme Zola, 'a very sweet and pleasant person', who seemed to know all about him, chatted civilly to him until her husband arrived. He too made a good impression, being 'not nearly so squat as he appears in his portrait'.[6] The portrait in question was almost certainly the engraving by De Liphart which had recently appeared in *La Vie moderne* and had been widely copied. It is the first of the many drawings made of Zola which show clearly the thickening of his body brought on by the sedentary life he was leading and his fondness for rich fare.

Gourmandise was a vice—as he called it—wickedly encouraged by his older friends Flaubert and Turgenev when they persuaded him to join them once a month in consuming a lavish dinner at one of the best restaurants in town. The company was limited to five, the other two being Daudet and, of course, Edmond de Goncourt, who described the first of these occasions in an unusually succinct diary entry for 14 April 1874: 'We started with a long discussion about the relative value of constipation and diarrhoea in literature; after that we passed on to the mechanism of the French language.'[7] These arguments about style, a subject on which Flaubert in particular was inexhaustible, used to astound Turgenev, who wrote French and spoke it with practised ease and to whom it had never occurred that a paragraph of prose needed to be chiselled and polished to a point of impossible perfection. But when the talk turned to feminine psychology, then Turgenev felt himself on firmer ground. Sprawling round a table in a private room, Flaubert and Zola in their shirt-sleeves, Turgenev with his gouty leg propped up on a divan, they would tell one

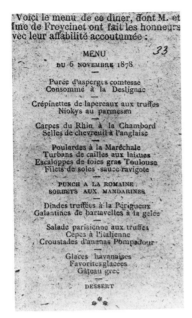

Voici le menu de ce dîner, dont M. et
Ime de Freycinet ont fait les honneurs
vec leur affabilité accoutumée :

MENU   33
DU 6 NOVEMBRE 1878

Purée d'asperges comtesse
Consommé à la Deslignac

Crépinettes de lapereaux aux truffes
Niokys au parmesan

Carpes du Rhin à la Chambord
Selles de chevreuil à l'anglaise

Poulardes à la Maréchale
Turbans de cailles aux laitues
Escaloppes de foies gras Toulouse
Filets de soles sauce ravigote

PUNCH A LA ROMAINE
SORBETS AUX MANDARINES

Dindes truffées à la Périgueux
Galantines de bartavelles à la gelée

Salade parisienne aux truffes
Cèpes à l'italienne
Croustades d'ananas Pompadour

Glaces havanaises
Favorites glacées
Gâteau grec

DESSERT

34 A contemporary menu, showing the kind of fare consumed by Flaubert and his
friends at their monthly dinner parties

another stories which Zola feared would have a disastrous effect on the
waiters' morals. He himself uttered some strange confidences in this
relaxed atmosphere, if we are to believe what Goncourt reported: that he
had 'no moral sense' and had slept with the wives of his best friends, or
that he was 'plagued by the desire to go to bed with a very young
girl—not a child, but a girl who had not yet reached puberty. "Yes," he
added, "it scares me . . . I can see myself being hauled before the courts
and God knows what else." '[8] Was there a Humbert buried deep somewhere in the more shadowy recesses of Zola's libido? In the shreds and
tatters of these indiscreetly recorded disclosures, made in the early hours
when rich food and rare wines had broken down the normal inhibitions,
braggadocio played no doubt quite as large a part as genuine self-
revelation.

There were in the late 1870s other literary dinner parties of a very
different kind, the oddly named 'dîners du Bœuf nature' held at the Café
Procope, at which Zola presided over a group of younger admirers and
disciples who included Paul Alexis, Céard, Huysmans, and Paul Bourget,
with from time to time Cézanne and other old friends from Aix, Antony
Valabrègue and Marius Roux. The presence of Paul Bourget, in later life a
pillar of the right-wing establishment, may seem surprising, but
L'Assommoir had impressed him as something totally new in literature,
something neither Balzac nor Flaubert nor Dickens had or could have
achieved. As for the first three named, they were all young men who had

read Zola's early works with admiration and had found some pretext or another to introduce themselves to him.

Only one of them came from Aix: this was Paul Alexis, who started his studies at the Lycée Bourbon the year Zola left it to go to Paris. After his departure a kind of legend had grown up at school about this brilliant alumnus, and when *Contes à Ninon* was published, a copy was surreptitiously handed round in class. For these boys from middle-class homes, the path Zola had chosen beckoned to them as a possible way of eluding the depressing destiny that awaited them otherwise—that of the briefless barrister or the clerk indentured to some country notary. Alexis was more determined than most to escape such a fate and one day, taking his courage in both hands, he left home clandestinely and bought a ticket for Paris. Almost the first thing he did when he arrived there was to ask his old school-friend Valabrègue to take him to see Zola, who gave him a cordial welcome and from nine that evening till one in the morning talked unstoppably about his plans for *Les Rougon-Macquart*, then only just finalized.

From that memorable evening in September 1869 dated the lifelong friendship that bound Alexis to the man who, in his eyes, could do no wrong either in his private life or in the domain of literature. Alexis never became a great writer himself; he scraped a living as a freelance journalist, published a few volumes of short stories, and collaborated in the confection of a few unimportant plays; but his most widely read book was the biography of Zola which he published in 1882. Zola's enemies denounced it as just one more instance of the man's incurable vanity; to get one of his disciples to write his biography when he was only forty-two, what presumption! Alexis was naïvely surprised at this reaction; all he had done, surely, was to try and satisfy public curiosity about his hero, a man he did not doubt for a moment was the greatest living writer in France.

In the early post-war period both Huysmans and Henry Céard were working as civil servants in different ministries. A shared admiration for Flaubert's work, *L'Education sentimentale*, first brought them together, and then Huysmans discovered Zola's works. Céard, having ferreted out the novelist's address, walked up to his Batignolles house one Sunday and passed in his card. There was some initial confusion, Zola having jumped to the conclusion that his visitor was trying to book an order for wine—the card showed that Céard was living at Bercy, well known as a depot for the wine trade. But once Céard mentioned the name of his friend Huysmans, Zola's expression lightened. Huysmans had just published his first work of fiction, *Marthe*, the short and simple story of the life of a prostitute, which had much moved Zola when he read it. So Céard was invited to call again at a more convenient hour and bring his friend with him.

In the summer of 1878, instead of taking his holidays by the seaside as had by now become his custom, Zola scoured the countryside round Paris

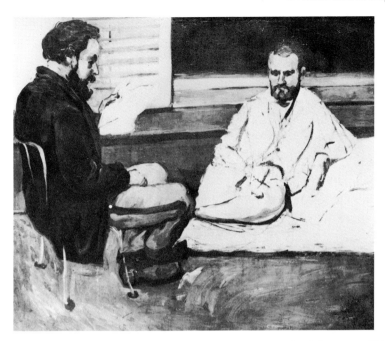

35 Cézanne's painting of Zola listening to Alexis reading aloud from one of his manuscripts

looking for a suitable house to rent near enough to allow him to come into the city on occasion and visit the Great Exhibition, the first to be held since 1867. His Russian readers were sure to want to know about it, and in fact Zola finally wrote no fewer than three articles on the subject for the *European Herald*. At a tiny riverside hamlet called Medan he found a secluded villa standing empty in an acre or so of ground and fell in love with it. Inquiries revealed, however, that the proprietor was not interested in a short-term lease so, with some of the royalties accruing from *L'Assommoir*, Zola bought it outright. It was small but well designed, and before long he threw out an extra wing and put up outhouses. Médan— the name came more easily off the tongue when the first vowel was sharpened—became his country retreat, his *dacha*, his Croisset; though he retained a commodious rented establishment in Paris for the winter season.

Regularly, at week-ends, his disciples took the train to the nearest station and made their way to Médan; the little band included not just those we have mentioned, but another strapping young fellow with bushy moustaches whom Zola had first come across at Flaubert's Sunday afternoon reunions, sitting quietly listening to his elders and seldom venturing a remark of his own. This was Guy de Maupassant. Like Céard and Huysmans, he was earning his living as a minor civil servant and had so far not published anything, though it was understood that he was learning his trade as a writer under Flaubert's expert tuition. Nobody took him too seriously—he seemed more interested in rowing up and down the Seine and flirting with the village girls than in debating the principles of naturalism with the others.

Delighted though he was to be able to lavish hospitality on this 'band of brothers', Zola expected much more from them than simple moral support: he wanted them to produce—novels or successful plays—and the letters he wrote to them were full of admonishments to this effect. If naturalism was to grow into a powerful literary movement, it would need to be illustrated by an impressive series of works, and so far only Huysmans had any kind of an established reputation. Partly in order to get the others known, partly in order to advertise the unity and cohesion of the new school, he suggested they should collaborate in a volume of short stories which should all deal with the same subject—the Franco-Prussian War. He himself had a story ready; it had been published some years earlier in Russian translation in *The European Herald*. Put on their mettle, the others turned to and on a given evening, each read out what he had written. The theatre director Antoine recalled Zola telling him, in almost the last year of his life, that when Maupassant had finished reading his story, *Boule de Suif*, 'everyone had the feeling that this was a masterpiece; their delight showed itself in congratulations and bear hugs rare enough between men of letters'.[9] Once it was published along with the others in the composite volume called *Soirées de Médan*, in April 1880, the public at large confirmed this opinion, and Maupassant was launched on his meteoric career as the one short-story writer of genius that France had ever produced.

For Zola the year 1880 was one of public triumph but also of private grief. The ninth volume of the *Rougon-Macquart* series, *Nana*, appeared in March, causing an even bigger sensation than *L'Assommoir*; anticipating, correctly, a record-breaking demand, Charpentier ordered a first printing of 55,000, a figure almost unheard of at the period. It is true that the publication of the novel had been preceded by a fanfare of publicity verging on vulgarity. Jules Laffitte, editor of the recently founded newspaper *Le Voltaire*, had acquired serialization rights and proceeded to make sure that everyone knew about this: he embarked on an advertising campaign which outdid Barnum in stridency. To get over his simple message: 'Read *Nana*! Read *Le Voltaire*!' he took space in other papers, placarded every available empty wall, and had his posters stuck on the sides of trams and of the cylindrically shaped urinals which were then so common in Paris. If neon lights had been invented, *Lisez Nana*! would have twinkled in the main square of every town in France from Bordeaux to Nancy. As it was, Laffitte made great use of sandwich men, a form of advertisement now happily obsolete. It was something of a scandal, or so felt, at any rate, even by those who were closest to Zola. 'Along the boulevards and the streets,' Maupassant wrote to Flaubert, 'can be seen

36 'The Birth of Nana-Venus', contemporary cartoon

men in overalls walking in single file holding banners on which can be read: "*Nana*, by Emile Zola, in the *Voltaire!*" If anyone asked me if I were a man of letters, I should answer: "No, sir, I sell fishing-rods", so humiliating for all of us do I find this insane advertising.'[10] Even Alexis was a little troubled, and wrote an article on *Nana* long before its serialization was completed solely in order to point out that the author of a novel cannot be held responsible for what a newspaper publisher does to try and increase his circulation figures.

Hardly had this uproar died down when a curt telegram reached Zola from Maupassant announcing Flaubert's death. This sudden disappearance of a man he had not merely admired but had grown to love over the years he had known him affected Zola deeply; but it was nothing like the wrench he suffered when, on 17 October, his mother died. She had brought him up, had been his constant companion in the years of adversity, and had lived to see him achieve the fame and riches for which her husband had toiled but which had eluded him all his life. Her last years had, all the same, been clouded by nervous illness, and the earlier good-humoured relations between her and her daughter-in-law had grown a little sour. Now, for the rest of his life, Emile and Alexandrine were to live side by side together, in that house at Médan or in their apartment in Paris, both places too big for the childless couple that they were and, it seemed, now always would be.

11 The Lure of the Stage

A point that cannot fail to strike anyone who studies the lives of the great artistic geniuses of western Europe, from Goethe onwards, is how seldom they seemed content to limit themselves to the particular speciality for which they were most obviously gifted. Blake was not happy to be just a poet, nor Wagner to be no more than a composer; similarly, Zola disliked being thought unqualified to do anything but write novels. It is as though the Renaissance ideal of the 'universal man' went on reverberating down the ages, and that the protean activities of giants like Michelangelo and Leonardo da Vinci continued to mesmerize their successors in the nineteenth and twentieth centuries. In France the nearest equivalent to these versatile artists of the cinquecento was no doubt Victor Hugo: not just the most prolific of romantic poets but also an innovatory playwright, a widely read novelist, a man active in the political field too and even unusually gifted as a graphic artist.

Zola, who had responded with some fervour to Hugo's lyric and dramatic genius in his youth, grew in time a little impatient of the exaggerated reverence paid to the old poet. When he first came to Paris, in 1858, Hugo was living in exile in Guernsey and, as Zola said, appeared to the young men of his own generation as 'a colossus in chains, whose harmonious voice could still be heard above the raging storm; he was Prometheus, he was the superman, he dominated France, surveying it from afar with his eagle's eye.'[1] But when, after his old enemy Louis-Napoleon had been driven from the throne, Hugo returned in triumph to France, Zola did not join with those who extended him a deliriously ecstatic welcome. For by now he had turned his back on romanticism, and viewed Hugo as the sole surviving representative of that outdated literary movement, who risked in his old age, especially if so thoughtlessly adulated, becoming a barrier against further progress. The mystical vein he appeared to be exploiting in his latest works seemed to Zola utterly incompatible with the modern scientific spirit; and besides, Hugo was unjustly monopolizing critical attention. Zola compared him to a giant sponge 'which, thanks to its absorbent properties, sucks in everything around it and so takes on swollen proportions'.[2]

This disobliging comparison was made in the course of a conversation with an interviewing journalist shortly after the publication of *Nana*; and it may be that he had been stung by certain disparaging remarks made by Hugo about *L'Assommoir*, which had reached his ears. Hugo had maliciously pretended to be under the impression that *L'Assommoir* was

37 A theatre audience of the period. The artist has depicted several celebrities in the stalls, including Zola (shown standing, full face, in front of one of the boxes)

really a novel translated from the Italian, and that this accounted for its stylistic peculiarities. More seriously, he contended that no author had the right to coin money by describing the sufferings of the poor. That these remarks, reported to Zola, exasperated him to the point of turning him into a sworn enemy of the 'Grand Old Man' of the French literary scene, seems to be confirmed by the extraordinarily bitter public attack he made on Hugo when the Théâtre-Français staged a revival of *Ruy Blas* in 1879. While conceding that the play glittered with lyrical splendour, he insisted waspishly that Hugo's psychology was puerile and his underlying philosophy corrupt. 'In spite of the beating wings of the verse, one cannot blink the facts: the plot is not merely crazy, it is immoral; the play could never inspire anyone to noble deeds, since the characters commit only foul or felonious ones; it provides neither uplift nor consolation, since it starts in mud and ends in blood.'[3] One could almost suppose that Zola pieced together this diatribe by cannibalizing the more virulent reviews that had been made of his own novels, beginning with *Thérèse Raquin*.

Ruy Blas was the last successful verse play Hugo had written; its original production dated back to 1838. The efforts that he, and a couple of close friends, Alexandre Dumas and Alfred de Vigny, had made to overthrow the outworn conventions of neoclassicism and establish a new, spirited, richly coloured romantic drama were by now legendary; the crusade, with its memorable battles against the bigoted pundits of the Academy, the over-cautious officials of the royal censorship, and the obstinately unco-operative actors and actresses of the Comédie Française, had taken place long before Zola was born. But he had read about it, no doubt, in the *Histoire du romantisme* that Théophile Gautier published in 1872 and, of course, the text of Hugo's plays (*Hernani, Marion de Lorme, Le Roi s'amuse,* besides *Ruy Blas* itself) was familiar to him since his school-days at Aix. In his more euphoric moments he dreamed of re-enacting this glorious campaign, of fighting some updated 'battle of *Hernani*', though the problems confronting him and his friends were not, of course, the same as Hugo and Dumas had faced. For those pioneers, the objective had been to destroy the crusty tradition of the serious five-act tragedy, based usually on plots borrowed from the history of ancient Rome, and written according to the rules laid down by Boileau in the seventeenth century and reformulated by La Harpe at the end of the eighteenth. Now, in the 1870s, what needed to be done was to loosen the hold that the 'well-made play' maintained over the theatre audiences of the time. Under the Second Empire a trio of talented but limited dramatists, Augier, Sardou, and Dumas *fils* (the son of the Dumas who had been Hugo's stalwart companion in his youth) had perfected a tradition of slick thesis playwriting that pandered to all the dreary prejudices of their middle-class patrons. Of one thing Zola was sure: something more red-blooded was needed. Why should he not be the man to provide it, sweeping the theatre clear of the dusty conventions that encumbered it, just as he had renovated the novel and enlarged its range with the publication of such works as *Thérèse Raquin* and *L'Assommoir* ?

Zola's theatrical ambitions did not, however, suddenly take shape in the 1870s when the idea occurred to him of repeating, with variations, Hugo's earlier feat. His interest in the stage dated back to his boyhood. There had been a small theatre at Aix, which opened its doors three times a week; as often as he had the price of a ticket in his pocket, young Emile would cheerfully forgo his supper in order to be first in the queue. There were play-readings too, with Cézanne and Baille, and even before he left Aix Zola had started composing short sketches in dialogue form. Alexis records having seen the manuscript of a farce completed when Zola was sixteen, about a successful attempt on the part of two schoolboys to supplant a *pion* in the affections of his girl-friend. At the Lycée Saint-Louis much of his spare time went on writing or planning other dramatic works: a play in verse on a medieval subject and a couple of one-act comedies, also in verse, rather similar to the curtain-raisers that Musset had written to illustrate well-known proverbs.

It is entirely possible that if, in his beginnings, Zola had received any encouragement to do so, he would have concentrated on writing for the stage and might never have considered becoming a novelist. Some time in 1865 he put the finishing touch to a one-act play, *La Laide*, about which he felt confident enough to try and get it accepted at one of the leading Paris theatres. Cannily, instead of submitting it directly to the management, he asked a young playwright, Adolphe Belot, to handle the matter for him. Belot owed him a good turn, for Zola had given one of his novels a favourable review in the Lyons newspaper, *Le Salut public*, to which he was contributing a book column at the time. Having read the sketch, Belot wrote advising Zola that in his view, despite its considerable dramatic merits, it stood little chance of acceptance, since even as a curtain-raiser it was rather too insipid and sentimental for modern tastes. *La Laide* is about the two daughters of a blind man who believes them to be equally beautiful; one is attractive though frivolous, the other a plain Jane full of estimable qualities and it is she, 'la Laide', whom the more eligible of the two young suitors chooses for his bride.

Belot suggested that this trifle might work better if Zola would take the trouble to rewrite it in verse. Too impatient, probably, to accept this well-meant advice, Zola insisted on its being sent just as it was to the manager of the Odéon who, as Belot had foreseen, rejected it. Undaunted, he set to work on a totally different kind of play: this was *Madeleine*, a gloomy melodrama which, as we have already suggested, may have been partly inspired by the earlier adventures of his mistress Alexandrine-Gabrielle Meley. This time, however, it appeared he had gone too far in the other direction. The manager of the Théâtre du Gymnase returned him the manuscript, telling him it was quite out of the question to stage his play; no audience would stand even the first act, let alone the other two, which were even more distressing.

These two successive rebuffs seem to have convinced Zola for the time being that he had better concentrate on writing novels. The notoriety he achieved with *Thérèse Raquin* confirmed him in this opinion, and instead of persisting in his efforts to get *Madeleine* accepted as a play, he rewrote it as a novel, *Madeleine Férat*, expanding it of course but introducing no radical changes. The theme—a woman who cannot escape her past—remained the same, and Zola had no need even to invent extra characters. The ease with which the play was turned into a work of fiction is evidence that, whatever he was writing, Zola instinctively adopted a dramatic structure.

Conversely, this meant that no insuperable difficulties arose when he wanted to extract a play from one of his novels, and in fact it was with a dramatized version of *Thérèse Raquin*, drafted some five years after the publication of the novel, that Zola first broke into the closed world of the theatre. Structurally, *Thérèse Raquin* was so eminently suited to recasting as a stage play that it has even been suggested that Zola might have had the possibility of such a conversion in mind when he drew up his plans for the novel. The strong impression conveyed that the characters are the pawns of fate gives it a superficial affinity with a Racinian tragedy, as too does the confinement of the action to a single setting, the 'dark damp chamber',[4] as Zola called it in his preface, above the Raquins' shop.

Modestly, Zola offered his play to none of the big Paris theatres, but to the Théâtre de la Renaissance, the manager of which, Hippolyte Hostein, discouraged by a series of failures, was rumoured to be on the point of closing down. Even so, Hostein was at first doubtful whether he should stake any of his dwindling capital on this melodrama by a newcomer, and was only persuaded to do so when a great actress, Marie Laurent, offered to take the part of Mme Raquin. Well supported by the rest of the cast, she helped carry it off though, having been put on at the extreme end of the season, *Thérèse Raquin* had only a short run in 1873. However, Marie Laurent subsequently took it abroad, and it was widely acclaimed in Germany and Scandinavia. There is, indeed, a distinct anticipatory flavour of Ibsen in *Thérèse Raquin*, traceable to the presence of a vital, strong-willed heroine (Thérèse) and to the firm construction moving remorselessly towards the catastrophe, features characterising all Ibsen's plays in the series that started with *A Doll's House* (1879) and culminated in *Hedda Gabler* (1892). This was partly why, when *Thérèse Raquin* was revived at the Théâtre du Vaudeville in May 1892, it did not appear to the theatre-goers of that time to be as dated as they might have expected.

Greatly encouraged by the serious attention the theatre critics gave his play, Zola took time off from his work on *La Faute de l'abbé Mouret*, the following year, in order to write a new one, a comedy called *Les Héritiers Rabourdin*, which he described as a pastiche of Molière, though the plot was actually adapted from Ben Jonson's *Volpone*. This time he lacked the advantage of being interpreted by an actress of the calibre of Marie Laurent; the cast was, in fact, mediocre, but even so the applause on the first night was gratifying. The critics, however, tore it to pieces the following day, complaining in particular about the sick-room atmosphere of the play, which is based on the situation of a ruined tradesman who knows he is dying but retains enough strength to pretend his business is flourishing and to extort presents from his relatives who expect to be repaid in the form of large legacies. The adverse notices in the press, to Zola's fury, kept the audiences away, and the play had to be taken off after only seventeen performances. Flaubert had predicted the result, telling his friend, after the successful first night: 'Tomorrow, you will be a great novelist.'[5] He was referring ironically to the jealousy theatre critics habitually displayed whenever a novelist had the audacity to try and make a new reputation for himself as a playwright; the cobbler was told, in no uncertain terms, to stick to his last.

If *Les Héritiers Rabourdin* was birth-strangled, Zola's third play, *Le Bouton de Rose*, was an abortion, which he would have done better never to bring to the light of day. Having finished *L'Assommoir* at the end of November 1876 Zola decided, as a relaxation, to write a broad farce for Plunkett, the manager of the Théâtre du Palais-Royal, who had approached him with this unlikely request some time earlier. The plot was a modification of one of Balzac's earthy *Contes drolatiques*: on his wedding-night a hotel manager is called away on urgent business and asks his partner to make sure the bride does not misconduct herself; the husband is duly punished, though not too heavily, for his lack of confidence in his wife's virtue. On first reading the script Plunkett got cold feet and tried to wriggle out of the agreement; then, later in the summer of 1877, when *L'Assommoir* had brought Zola nation-wide celebrity, he changed his mind. Ironically, so did Zola: re-reading *Le Bouton de Rose* down at L'Estaque where he was holidaying, he came to the conclusion it would do his image no good to have the play performed, and wanted to withdraw it. However, Plunkett pressed him to authorize production and Zola weakly agreed. The event proved his instincts to have been correct. On the first night the comedy was mercilessly hissed and the angry audience refused to allow the leading actor to pronounce the name of the author after the final curtain, as was the custom. Nevertheless, Zola took all his friends off to Véfour's restaurant to eat what had been intended as a celebration supper but which turned out to be the funeral baked meats. It was an embarrassingly large party. Flaubert was there, sturdily declaiming against the objectors; so were Alphonse and Julia Daudet, the Charpentiers, Alexis, Céard, and Marius Roux, some of his artist friends including Manet and Guillemet, and of course Edmond de Goncourt, who described the occasion with malicious glee in his diary. Zola, utterly crushed, left it to his wife to order the meal, and sat at the head of the table, absently twiddling his knife between his fingers, and grunting disjointed phrases: 'No, I don't give a damn really, but all my programme of work will need to be changed . . . I shall have to go straight on to *Nana* now . . . Really, these flops, it's enough to put anyone off the theatre . . . *La Curée* will have to wait, I shall go back to the novels . . .'[6] By *La Curée* Zola meant the dramatized version of that novel which he eventually completed, as *Renée*, at the suggestion of Sarah Bernhardt, who then declined to take the title part.

From his successive experiences with *Thérèse Raquin*, *Les Héritiers Rabourdin*, and now *Le Bouton de Rose* Zola drew two conclusions: the first was that his best chance of making headway as a dramatist lay in turning his novels into plays; and the second, that in any future such enterprise it would be safer not to let his name appear as author or even co-author. Writing as a regular drama critic, first in *L'Avenir national* (1873) and later in *Le Bien public* (1876–8), Zola had stirred up a hornet's

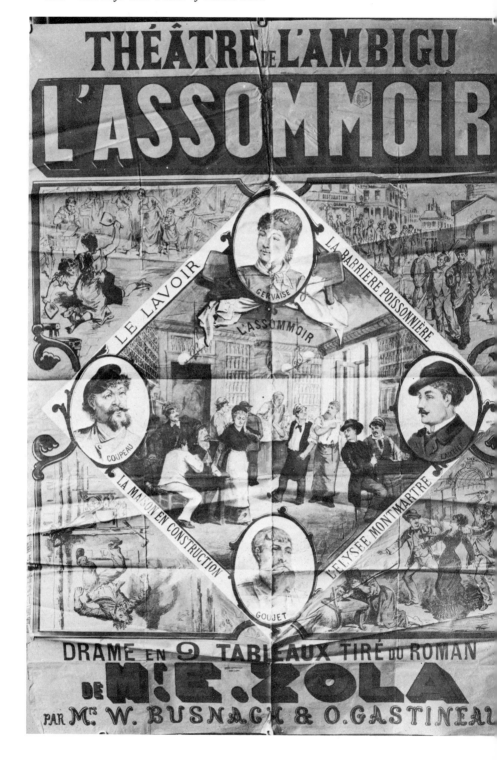

38 *Opposite* A playbill advertising *L'Assommoir*
39 *Above* Gervaise (played by Hélène Petit) and Coupeau, in one of the opening
scenes of Busnach's adaptation of *L'Assommoir*, photographed by Nadar

nest of enemies among those with a vested interest in maintaining the flow
of trivia that passed in those days for theatrical entertainment, and if he
was to bring his campaign to a successful conclusion he would need to
proceed by stealth and camouflage his approach.

The opportunity presented itself quite soon. *L'Assommoir* had been so
widely read and discussed since its publication that it was almost bound to
occur to someone to cash in on its fame by turning it into a stage-play;
had the same thing happened sixty or seventy years later there would have
been a rush for the film rights. Zola had already been approached by a
couple of well-known dramatists, one of them Sardou, and had turned

down their proposals, when he received a visit from an obscure writer of vaudevilles, William Busnach. Busnach had already called on him once before, when *L'Assommoir* was still appearing in instalments in *La République des Lettres*; he had been so taken by the novel that, too impatient to await the successive parts as they came out week by week, he begged the editor, Catulle Mendès, to give him a letter of introduction to the author who, he hoped, would allow him to read the still unpublished part of the work in manuscript. Busnach's subsequent request for authority to turn *L'Assommoir* into a serious play seemed to Zola so strange, coming from a writer of lightweight song-and-dance entertainments, that he demurred at first, until Busnach sent him a scenario. Then he allowed himself to be persuaded, sensing that the awe in which the younger man held him would make him an easy-going associate to deal with. However, he left the writing of the dialogue entirely to Busnach, though he may have had some hand in the revamping of the plot. In order to make it more acceptable to the ordinary playgoer certain changes were made both in the motivation of the characters and in their psychology. Gervaise, in particular, is transformed into a loyal and faithful wife, in spite of her brute of a husband, and does not, as in the novel, succumb to the temptation of drink. All her misfortunes are due to the hateful machinations of her rival Virginie, who is even made responsible for Coupeau's fall at work which in the novel was a pure accident.

These alterations turned *L'Assommoir* into something very close to the traditional melodrama, with a pure-hearted, pathetic heroine persecuted by an assortment of villains of both sexes. Hélène Petit, as Gervaise, scored a great personal triumph, and the play as a whole was a sensational box-office success, with an initial run of three hundred performances; after which two separate companies toured the provinces with it, playing everywhere to full houses. Those who had read the book flocked to see the play, and those who had not, having seen the play, rushed out to buy their copy of the book. News of the production spread abroad, and Charles Reade was commissioned to provide an English version. Entitled starkly *Drink*, it was first shown at the Princess's Theatre on 7 June 1879, less than six months after the original play had opened in Paris. Charles Warner's virtuoso acting in the delirium tremens scene brought the house down and Bernard Shaw stated that, aesthetic merits apart, the play had 'as a matter of simple fact, deterred many young men from drunkenness'.[7] Zola too did not hesitate to underscore the moral lesson of Busnach's play. 'If the theatre is meant to mend manners, the doors of the Ambigu should be thrown open to all comers, so that they can see what drink leads to.'[8]

Eventually Zola grew a little tired of all the ballyhoo surrounding this play, and flatly refused to attend the hundredth performance, an occasion marked by a fashionable costume ball at which all the guests were asked to arrive dressed as workmen or washerwomen. However, he did not refuse Busnach's plea to be allowed to dramatize his next best-seller, *Nana*,

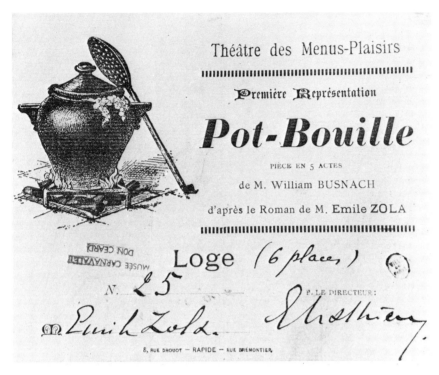

Théâtre des Menus-Plaisirs

IIIIIIIIIIIIIIIIIIIIIIIIIIIIIIIIIIIIIIIIIIIIIIIIIIIIIIIIIIII

Première Représentation

Pot-Bouille

PIÈCE EN 5 ACTES

de M. William BUSNACH

d'après le Roman de M. Emile ZOLA

IIIIIIIIIIIIIIIIIIIIIIIIIIIIIIIIIIIIIIIIIIIIIIIIIIIIIIIIIIII

Loge (6 places)

N. 25

P. LE DIRECTEUR:

8, RUE DROUOT — RAPIDE — RUE BRÉMONTIER.

40 Zola's ticket for a performance of *Pot-Bouille*

though he insisted this time on vetting the text. There was some disappointment at the extent to which the plot had been emasculated, and the attempts to achieve realism by the use of unusual stage effects (edible apples dropping from a pasteboard tree, and a real stream of water in a riverside scene) were judged ill-advised. Even so, the version notched over a hundred performances which, if less satisfactory than the record number reached by *L'Assommoir*, was well in excess of the runs achieved by any of the plays Zola had written himself.

Nana was followed by dramatizations of *Pot-Bouille* and *Le Ventre de Paris*, both attributed on the playbills solely to Busnach, though by now Zola was making no secret of the extent to which he was personally collaborating in these productions. 'I would like to be the man', he told an interviewing journalist, 'finally to let a gust of fresh air from real life blow through the backcloth. A revolution is bound to come, and I should like to lead it. That's my ambition.' He hoped to make it come true once he had completed the five remaining volumes of the *Rougon-Macquart* series. In the meantime, his collaboration with a talented professional like Busnach was giving him valuable experience; but, he repeated, the adaptions were not the realist drama he had in mind. 'Busnach and I are not at the moment engaged on the great popular revolution I dream of, and for

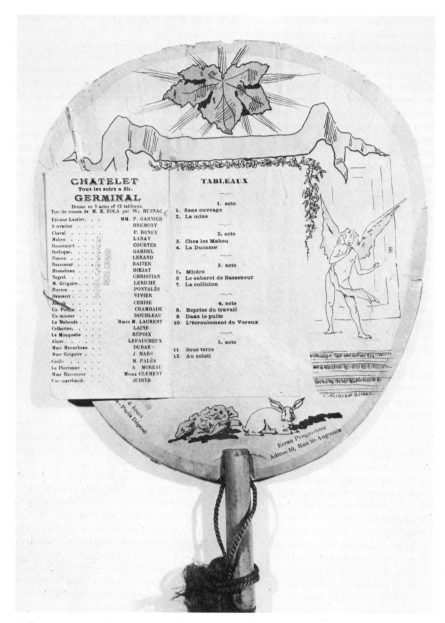

41 Programme of *Germinal*, sold affixed to a fan. Theatres at the time were often uncomfortably hot because of the numerous gas-lit chandeliers

which it would be necessary to apply all my ideas and nothing but my ideas.[9]

At the time these words were recorded, in February 1887, Zola's association with Busnach was near being dissolved. The last collaborative effort they embarked on was an adaptation of *Germinal* which ran into serious trouble. Zola insisted, this time, in doing nearly all the work himself; Busnach's role was reduced to that of an adviser. He was horrified at some of the scenes the novelist was proposing to show, and begged him to take his word for it that the play would never be licensed for public performance when it showed striking workmen being fired on by the police. Busnach was, of course, absolutely right; but Zola had the bit between his teeth and insisted on submitting the text as he had written it. What he seems to have wanted was a showdown with the authorities, and in particular with René Goblot, the minister principally concerned, over the whole question of the licensing system, a relic of earlier days of preventive censorship. He probably foresaw that the 'revolution in the theatre' of which he dreamed could never take place until the Bastille of the *commission d'examen* had been demolished. Goblot, having read the manuscript, was adamant: he would never permit the showing of so blatantly socialistic a play. Zola retaliated by sending an account of his dealings with Goblot and his staff to *Le Figaro*, which printed it on 29 October 1885; it counts as one of the best pieces of polemical prose he ever wrote, bubbling over with sardonic humour; but it did nothing to soften government resistance to the production of *Germinal*.

The play was eventually staged, after a three-year wait, and proved a dismal failure. Albert Wolff, one of Zola's most tenacious opponents, seized the opportunity to launch a devastating attack on his practice of sheltering behind Busnach's burly frame, letting him be a target for the brickbats when things went wrong and expecting him to fade into the background when the notices were good. Possibly Zola felt the justice of this criticism; or, more probably, he was mortified at the clear evidence that, as soon as he tried to plan and write a play unaided, it failed. At any rate he never collaborated with Busnach again, nor did he turn his hand to any new plays. The librettos he wrote towards the end of his life for Bruneau's operatic works fall into a different category of dramatic writing, and will be discussed in our concluding chapter.

12 Portrait of the Man

Zola's personal appearance is known to us through a variety of portraits made at different times in his life, some by painters, some by engravers and other illustrators, some again by photographers. Broadly speaking, these images can be said to fall into three distinct groups, as though Zola lived through three separate stages, each reflected in a different physical type. There is firstly the romantic youth that Cézanne and Manet painted in the 1860s, more candidly recorded in a full-length studio picture taken probably by a none-too-competent professional photographer when Zola was about twenty. Thick dark hair and what used to be called a Newgate frill—a fringe of beard running from ear to ear but scraped away from the cheeks and chin—encircle a sad little face, almost feminine in its wistfulness; the eyes gaze soulfully, the corners of the mouth are drawn down to give an expression not so much of grimness as of resigned melancholy. The second picture is of a man self-confident, solidly built, as aggressively pushful as, previously, he seemed shy, delicate and retiring. In the photographs taken in his late thirties and forties and in the caricatures that started to appear about the same time in the humorous papers, the hair is cut shorter and is not parted while the beard is full and includes a luxuriant moustache under which one can usually make out the same pouting lips, though their expression is different: disdainful rather than pathetic. The high forehead is already quite heavily lined and the caricaturists did not forget the two deep-cut grooves in the flesh on either side of his nose. Finally there is Zola in his fifties, a man so prematurely aged as to appear ten years older than he was and to be the grandfather in the family group in those snapshots that show him with his children and their mother. The beard and moustache are now grizzled, the hair, though still dark, is thinner and has receded further up the great dome of the forehead, while the eyes have acquired a pensive, often visionary look.

At no stage in his life could Zola's appearance be called impressive; in this respect he was among the least favoured of the major French writers of his century. He had nothing of Hugo's majestic presence and irresistible charm or of the virile magnetism that in his youth caused all eyes to be turned on Gustave Flaubert when he entered the theatre auditorium at Rouen. There was no counterpart to Baudelaire's sardonic stare, as keen as the guillotine's blade, nor to the lustrous, fascinating gaze that Balzac could turn on an interlocutor. Zola's eyes always appear veiled, for he was seriously short-sighted and had been so ever since the age of sixteen. In earlier life he used no artificial aids to correct his defective vision; this was

42 Zola aged about twenty

one of his very few touches of personal vanity. Later, nearly every picture shows him with a *lorgnette*, though he rarely permitted himself to be photographed wearing it; it dangles out of sight on the end of a thin cord hung round his collar, or else he is shown toying with it absently, as though it were a paper-knife he had chanced to pick up. Only the most hostile caricaturists depict him with the glasses actually perched on his nose. But this minor coquetry disappeared in time and every photograph taken in the last ten or fifteen years of his life features the characteristic *pince-nez* most weak-sighted gentlemen wore at this period.

43 Zola aged thirty-five

Zola's myopia, compounded by his refusal for many years to avail himself of the help a good optician could have given him, has been plausibly adduced as a reason for the peculiar indistinctness of many of the descriptive passages in his novels, especially where more distant panoramas are introduced; a kind of smoky haze hangs over things, the profusion of remote objects is translated in his prose as a jumbled flashing of sparks of colour. As one would expect, this feature is observable particularly in earlier novels like *La Curée* and *Le Ventre de Paris*; in a later work such as *La Terre*, written at a time when he had accustomed himself to wearing glasses out of doors, even distant details, a church spire on the horizon or scattered reapers on far-away fields, are shown as being clearly discernible. It is interesting too to speculate how far Zola's early admiration for some of the outdoor painters of his time depended on the quite fortuitous fact that their adoption of certain technical devices, such as twirls and blobs of colour, in order to convey a sense of immediacy or, sometimes, of swirling movement, corresponded closely to the way he himself normally saw objects at a certain distance. Later, with his *pince-nez* fixed on his nose, he no longer perceived sunlit nature as the shimmering mist it seemed to be in the landscapes of Renoir or in Monet's urban scenes, his painting of the Boulevard des Capucines for instance, in which the pedestrians appear as nondescript streaks; and it may well be significant that his progressive disenchantment with the work of the Impressionists, something we shall be examining in a later chapter, coincided approximately with his growing reliance on spectacles to provide him with a clearer vision of his surroundings. If contact lenses had been available in 1860, not only Zola's literary work but his art criticism too might well have evolved very differently.

It sometimes happens that when one sense is defective, another will acquire compensatory acuteness. If Zola registered the visual scene imper-

44 Zola towards the end of his life

fectly, he made up for this failure by a highly developed sense of smell. It was largely a question of memory; he was able to evoke at will the distinctive odour not just of each town he had visited, but often of particular streets or market-places at this or that season of the year. Smells may not have assailed his nostrils any more powerfully than they did the next man's but, like Baudelaire and Proust, he was extraordinarily sensitive to their evocative power. At a period when he had hardly enough money to buy food, he would spend his last coppers on a bunch of sweet peas and put them in a jar on his bedside table; 'and this faint perfume of orange-blossom', so he told Robert de Montesquiou, the chance recipient of this curious confidence, 'used to make me dream all night of my childhood'.[1] The alkaline smell of the live poultry kept underground in the cellars of Les Halles remained with him for a whole month after he was taken to see them in the course of an expedition to gather background material for *Le Ventre de Paris*. It is in this novel that one finds the most extravagant descriptive sequences devoted to characterizing different smells, like the notorious scene in the cheese store, where the peculiar odour of each cheese is denoted in terms of particular musical instruments combining in a weirdly cacophonous symphony. In this respect, the nearest equivalent to Zola among English novelists may well be John Cowper Powys, with his sensitivity to the strangely exciting effect of the smell of honeysuckle blending with that of pig manure and to the 'perilous, arrowy faintness' of the scent of primroses in a bowl of freshly picked wild flowers.

Contemporaries, noticing the frequency of olfactory descriptions in the *Rougon-Macquart* novels, supposed that Zola must have had a peculiarly constituted nose. It was, indeed, perhaps the most characteristic feature of his face. E. A. Vizetelly, his English translator and publisher, noticed Zola's nose when he first set eyes on him, in the reporters' gallery at Versailles in 1871; he called it 'curiously misshapen',[2] but in fact it was misshapen only in the sense that it was cleft at the tip. It was a highly mobile and expressive organ. Both Léon Daudet and Edmond de Goncourt likened it to the muzzle of a retriever, and the latter, in a vivid passage of his diary, referred to it as 'a questioning, approving, disapproving nose, a nose that can show gaiety or melancholy, a nose in which the physiognomy of its owner is concentrated'.[3]

Most of Zola's visitors, however, found they could read his mood better by watching his hands. After dining with him in the summer of 1888, André Antoine, the director of the experimental Théâtre Libre, was taken by Zola into his study and, sitting there listening to him, found his attention drawn particularly to his 'delicate, mobile, astonishingly expressive hands'.[4] The same observation was made by one of Antoine's closest friends, the architect and sculptor Frantz Jourdain, who pointed out that no photograph could do justice to Zola's hands, nor 'render their agitation, or more precisely their animation, the curious movement of the fingers when, for instance, stirring a spoon in a cup of tea'.[5] His state of mind could sometimes be deduced, too, from the movements of his foot, as happened on the memorable occasion when the English journalist R. H. Sherard ventured to take Oscar Wilde, with Lord Alfred Douglas in tow, to Zola's house and introduce the two men. As well introduce a cat to a mastiff. After the first few minutes it was obvious that the author of *La Débâcle* had nothing at all in common with the brilliantly erratic Irish aesthete, whose *Salomé* was being currently rehearsed in London with Sarah Bernhardt in the lead part. Zola's face, Sherard records, 'assumed a half-puzzled, half-suspicious air, as though he were in doubt whether some practical joke were not being played on him. He showed all those signs of extreme nervousness which were apparent when social observance was putting constraint upon him. I never saw him wag his foot more vigorously than on that occasion, and during the whole interview I was in fear that at any moment he might bring it to a close with that brusquerie which he could sometimes assume towards visitors who were not welcome to him.'[6]

Other callers were impressed by his attractive tenor voice, that 'charming voice with the resonance of a silver bell'[7] which Emile Bergerat, Gautier's son-in-law, was so surprised to hear, when he first met him, coming from a man of such plebeian appearance. But Zola was not a brilliant or even very adequate conversationalist. He lacked all the qualities summed up in the word *esprit* which the French valued so highly, and more highly then, no doubt, than they do now: playful paradox, the knowing allusion, the sparkling epigram. If he ever came across La Bruyère's definition of the truly sociable man—one who always ensures that the person he is talking to will be left with a good opinion of himself—he must have reflected that this was a gift he did not possess and could never aspire to. In mixed society he was mostly silent or, if he intervened, was apt to wade in with some flat or ponderous remark contrasting uncomfortably with the accepted flippancy of *salon* conversation. He was more at his ease when surrounded by younger disciples whom he felt to be broadly in sympathy with him. Then, as one of them (the Swiss novelist Edouard Rod) remarked, 'he could be very eloquent. His conversation would open out on some subject and he would dip lightly into it, affording rich glimpses, scattering in profusion bold ideas and suggestive criticisms, which fixed and retained the attention.'[8] Journalists who had arranged to interview him on some topic of the hour were often surprised by a flow of words that seemed designed less to convince them of the rightness of his point of view than to formulate it for himself. He seemed on such occasions to be hardly aware of the person he was addressing but to be talking, as one of them said, 'like a student who has crammed a subject for an examination'.[9]

It might be thought that such a man, so ready to talk and so reluctant to converse, would make an ideal public speaker. But however strongly he was tempted, at certain periods of his life, to enter politics, he knew that such a career was ruled out by the excessive nervousness that made the very thought of delivering a speech a nightmare for him. The furthest he ventured along this path was to accept nomination for the presidency of the Société des Gens de Lettres, a step taken deliberately in order to force himself to speak in public. He was duly elected in 1891 and chaired all the Society's meetings. But when, two years later, he was invited in his official capacity to come to London and address the corresponding British institution (the Society of Authors), he wrote his speech out in advance and learnt it off by heart, rehearsing it before going to bed for several nights before the occasion. Then, when the great moment arrived, stage fright took over; he pulled the paper out of his pocket and read out his speech.

Such diffidence cannot be entirely accounted for by the combination in Zola of extreme introversion with an unusually lively imagination, which painted to him in the most lurid colours dire intimations of disaster. His timidity, humourlessness and constraint in company were symptomatic of something else: an over-controlled psyche. The novels, with their occasionally ghastly, morbidly gloomy, or hotly sensual scenes, were the normal outlet for all those suppressed desires and dissimulated phobias that churned endlessly in his subconscious; but sometimes this literary safety-valve failed to function adequately, and then Zola was liable to succumb to severe fits of nervous prostration. Most authors experience a certain depressive reaction on completing a book that has taxed their faculties to the limit; in Zola's case the reaction could be severe enough to oblige him to stay in bed for several days, suffering what he called 'abominable neurotic pains'.[10] In October 1882 he had a complete nervous breakdown, from which he emerged feeling 'abominably tired. . . . I really need to spend two or three years free of all mental work so as to get my strength back. The novel I am due to finish terrifies me, I have grown such a coward.'[11]

These confidences were made to Henry Céard, who has left on record some curious instances of Zola's quasi-feminine sensibility. He mentions an occasion when he saw him quite sick, in his Rue de Boulogne apartment, after coming in from witnessing a street accident, a man decapitated by the wheels of a tramcar. Céard also remembered seeing him enter one of the Impressionist exhibitions in a state of abject terror, pale and trembling and looking for somewhere to hide; a summer thunderstorm had burst overhead and every flash of lightning streaking across the black sky made him flinch painfully.

Even in ordinary circumstances, his hypersensitivity manifested itself in a dozen different ways. He had only to prick his finger to suffer severe shooting pains in the arm. The pressure of a tight-fitting garment caused him agony, and one of his first requests to a friend who came across from Paris when he was living in hiding in England was that his visitor should bring him a parcel of shirts on his next trip over, those in the London shops being far too narrowly cut for Zola's comfort. His adoption of the loose flowing peasant smock when working at home was no concession to populism but simply a consequence of his dislike of constricting clothing.

Overwork could bring on attacks of neuralgia which had no recognizable organic origin. Sometimes he complained of his heart racing, of kidney trouble; there was a time when he needed to urinate so frequently that he took to keeping a chamber-pot under his desk. The Goncourt diary records twice, at an interval of ten years, how at dinner Zola's hands trembled so badly that he could hardly raise his glass to his lips without spilling the wine.

Hypochondria afflicted him particularly around his fortieth year, and was aggravated, but not actually triggered off, by the bereavements he suffered in 1880 and by the deaths of Manet and Turgenev in 1883. But it was a condition he had suffered from since early manhood. In some of the letters he wrote to his friends at Aix when he was twenty he voices complaints about 'some physical disorder or other about which no doctor can give me a satisfactory account. My digestive system is profoundly affected. I feel a heaviness in the stomach and bowels; sometimes I feel I could eat an ox, at other times I can't touch food at all.'[12] In one form or another, this neurotic condition continued all his life with, of course, periods of intermission. It made nonsense of the popular view of him as 'a thick-skinned plough animal, with coarse senses, plodding along mechanically, motivated solely by a crude desire for profit'.[13] These bitter words were Zola's own and occur in the preface he penned for a monograph written by Edmond Toulouse, a professor of psychiatric medicine who, in 1896, gave him a thorough physical and psychological examination and published the results in this book. Zola commended it as the work of an impartial scientist, embodying the unassailable, objectively established facts, and added that he had consented to its publication in the hope that it might help destroy the popular myth. The truth was that, far from having a thick hide, he was the most thin-skinned of men, 'shuddering and suffering in the slightest breath of air, sitting down every morning to write his daily stint in a state of anguish, carrying out his work only by means of a constant struggle of the will against self-doubt'.[14]

We shall see in our next chapter how this 'daily stint' was accomplished, and how painfully the monumental edifice of *Les Rougon-Macquart* was raised by its architect who, in spite of all the encouragement that world-wide renown and a princely income from sales could give him, never managed to rid himself of the feeling that what he was doing was pointless and that what he sought to do was utterly beyond his powers.

13 Portrait of the Writer

Between 1871 and Zola's death in 1902 one can count only six years when no new novel issued from his pen. Over these thirty-one years he published, in addition, eight volumes of critical essays or polemical pieces, three volumes of short stories, and a collection of plays. As a record of productivity this is, of course, far from unique; several other nineteenth-century writers rivalled or surpassed it: Balzac, George Sand, Anthony Trollope, Alexandre Dumas and Jules Verne, to name but a few. But whereas, for most of these, writing came as easily as spawning to a fish, the case was different with Zola. Whenever he was asked about it, he always spoke feelingly of the agonized toil his novels cost him; the language he used customarily involved a comparison with the discomfort and pain undergone by a woman during confinement. The moment of conception may have been joyful, but the long months of gestation were as burdensome as a period of pregnancy. Even when the last word was written, there was no real sense of delivery, for after that there were the proofs to correct and by the time the volume came off the presses he was sick of it and wanted only to forget about it. If obliged, years later, to re-read part of one of his novels to remind himself of certain details, he never felt the glow of satisfaction with which some more fortunate authors were able to contemplate a finished work; on the contrary, he found himself groaning in despair at its inadequacies.

Writing came most easily to him when his head 'seemed to be empty', as he put it, and ideas swam slowly to the surface to arrange themselves in a logical order. A torrent of inspiration was a positive embarrassment, for then he could not find the words he wanted, and what he did put down on paper seemed third-rate. If he persisted, struggling with a rebellious passage, the effort could actually cause him to have an erection. But there were other occasions when he would sit down at his desk at the usual time in the morning to write the next few pages of the work in hand, and find that everything had gone blank; it was as though he were lost in a dense black fog which prevented him from visualizing the scene or the characters. When this happened there was nothing he could do but cup his chin in his hand and stare desperately out of the window, like a man who had lost his memory and was struggling to recapture some small detail from the past that would enable him to reconstruct the present.

But for all this, Zola never started a novel that he did not finish, as happened to Balzac and, even more frequently, to Stendhal. Stendhal, apparently, wrote or dictated his novels—those that he completed at

45 Zola seated at his huge desk in the study at Médan

least—straight off, with very little conscious preparation; 'to draw up a plan', he used to say, 'freezes the current of inspiration'. Zola's practice was the direct opposite: he planned each novel down to the minutest particular, firstly in broad outline, then chapter by chapter. The purpose was partly to ensure a firmly logical structure, and partly to give himself confidence. Zola hated navigating in uncharted waters, just as Stendhal hated to set sail unless for a voyage over unknown seas.

Normally he would start knowing only which particular member of the

Rougon-Macquart family was to be the hero or heroine of the new novel, and what, broadly speaking, its theme was to be. The first task he set himself was to work out a viable plot which would allow the subject to be adequately treated. This was done pen in hand, and since Zola's work-sheets have mostly been preserved, the manuscripts provide us with a unique record of the meanderings, false starts and sudden inspirational leaps of a creative writer's imagination. It is remarkable how frequently, in the very first sentence of these sketches or *ébauches* as Zola called them, he uses the word 'poem', suggesting that his work may derive more directly from the epics of ancient days than from the stage comedy out of which the novel of manners or *roman de mœurs* is usually considered to have developed. Thus, the *ébauche* of *La Terre* opens with the statement: 'I want to write the living poem of the earth, but in its human rather than symbolic aspect.'[1] When he began putting his ideas together for the novel centred on the creation of a big modern departmental store, a sort of Parisian Harrods, Zola opens his file with a similar statement of intent: 'I want, in *Au Bonheur des Dames*, to write the poem of modern [commercial] activity.'[2] *Nana* is to be 'the poem of man's sexual desire, the great lever that lifts the world'.[3] The plot, and the characters, were invented to give the 'poem' its indispensable narrative structure, and we can watch him in these sketches experimenting with different ways of doing this.

He rarely succeeded at a first attempt in constructing an outline plot that satisfied him. An early draft plan for *Nana* was scrapped because he considered it was awkwardly reminiscent of part of Balzac's *La Cousine Bette*. He made no fewer than four attempts to work out a viable plot for *La Joie de vivre* in 1880, gave up in despair and started a quite different novel (*Pot-Bouille*), completed it and also its sequel, *Au Bonheur des Dames*, and then finally, three years after abandoning it, made a further attempt to fix the broad outlines of *La Joie de vivre*, this time successfully. The discarded plots seem no less promising than the plan he eventually adopted, but one must suppose they did not satisfy Zola's criteria for incarnating, in the most dramatic way possible, the central idea he wanted the book to convey.

As soon as a draft plan had been provisionally settled, Zola embarked on the next stage, which he called documentation. It was a process of fact-finding research carried out systematically in those areas of his subject on which he felt himself insufficiently informed. Thus, he had made up his mind that the central character of *La Faute de l'abbé Mouret* was to be a priest. But Zola's prior knowledge of the clerical world was extremely limited. He needed to find out, among other things, what kind of training was given to seminarists since he planned to refer in his novel to the repercussions on his hero, Serge Mouret, of his early education in a seminary. The priests he questioned were evasive; finally he was lucky enough to run to earth an unfrocked *abbé* who told him what he wanted to

46 When collecting materials for *Le Ventre de Paris* Zola paid a series of visits to the markets of Les Halles

know. It was also necessary to ascertain the exact sequence of formulae, movements and responses in the ceremony of the mass, since he planned to show Serge celebrating the Eucharist in his opening chapter. So, perhaps for the first time in his life, Zola attended divine service at his local church, Sainte-Marie des Batignolles, edifying the sparse congregation by his intense absorption in each stage of the mystic drama being enacted.

There was not a single one of the *Rougon-Macquart* novels for which Zola did not feel it necessary to 'document' himself in some degree. He was able to do some of this work at home or in libraries: reading up property law for *La Curée*, studying glossaries of workmen's slang for *L'Assommoir*, or leafing through medical treatises on miners' diseases for *Germinal*. Before writing his novel on the Franco-Prussian War, *La Débâcle*, he read a whole collection of memoirs written by soldiers or by civilians who had been caught up in the fighting. In addition, as a good journalist, Zola realized the value of personal investigation. When collecting material for *Le Ventre de Paris* he paid a series of visits to the Central Markets, notebook in hand, to record their appearance at different times of the day, in sunshine and in rain. He even spent a night there simply in order to see the provision carts arrive in the early hours to discharge the produce they had brought in from the market-gardens, and persuaded one of the inspectors to take him down into the cellars of Les Halles and show him round. A few years later, Vizetelly was intrigued to see Zola sitting on a sofa in the 'managerial corner of the ground-floor promenade' of the Folies Bergère, keeping an attentive eye on the chattering throng and taking copious notes, to the amusement of the 'passing *habituées*, who desired to know if he were drawing their portraits, or else insinuated that he was making out his washing-list'.[4] In fact, as the British journalist later discovered, he was gathering material for *Nana*.

He prided himself inordinately on the care he took to verify every detail he introduced into each of his books, and in the interviews he was always happy to grant to newspapermen anxious to do a profile of him, he would dwell complacently on this aspect of his method, insisting, a little misleadingly, that he 'invented nothing'. Thanks to the interest aroused by the newspaper articles that were written on the basis of these interviews, he found that in later years he encountered less suspicion and puzzlement on the part of officials when he approached them with special requests. The management of the Bon Marché, the store that served him as principal model for his emporium in *Au Bonheur des Dames*, raised no objection when he asked to be allowed to question the staff about their working conditions. Having decided that the hero of *La Bête humaine* should be an engine-driver, Zola made application to the managing director of the Western Railway Company and as a special favour was authorized to ride on the footplate of an engine making the run between Paris and Mantes. Interesting though this experience was, he was probably more effectively helped by the advice and information supplied by a traffic manager in the employ of the Company, one Pol Lefèvre.

When considering Zola's documentary methods, the most instructive case-history to examine is, however, *Germinal*. In the summer of 1883, while on holiday at a small resort near Quimper, he happened to make the acquaintance of a science teacher in the University of Lille, Alfred Giard, who also sat in the Chamber of Deputies as elected representative of the mining constituency of Valenciennes, near the Belgian frontier. At that time Zola had still to write the concluding chapters of *La Joie de vivre* and was reckoning to start next on his novel about a farming community, *La Terre*. But his conversations with Giard persuaded him to embark instead on the study of industrial conflict which he had intended for many years to use in one of the *Rougon-Macquart* novels, without being very clear what setting to choose. It was Giard who convinced him of the advantages of writing about a mining area, rather than a big factory or steelworks; the socialist deputy offered to conduct him round the Anzin coalfields whenever he wished. Zola remembered this offer when, on 19 February 1884, he read in the morning paper that a large-scale strike had just broken out in the area. Four days later he was on his way to Valenciennes. Giard, whom the miners trusted as a man who had their interests at heart, suggested to the novelist that he should pose as his secretary; this subterfuge would allay the suspicions of the strikers, who might have

47 A typical Second-Empire departmental store of the kind Zola described in *Au Bonheur des Dames*

48 Zola riding on the footplate of a locomotive between Paris and Mantes

handled him roughly if they had got the impression he was in the pay of the mining company. In this way Zola was able to talk freely to the leaders of the strike, sit in at union meetings, visit the miners' cottages, go down one of the pits in a steam-operated 'cage', in short see for himself what conditions were like for the pitmen, their wives and families, both on the surface and underground. Years later, Sherard ran across an old foreman in the Anzin district who told him he had never met a man who asked so many questions.

Once the process of documentation was completed, Zola returned to his draft plan, which sometimes needed to be modified in the light of what he had learned. After the main lines of the action of his novel were finally established he drew up a kind of synopsis, chapter by chapter, and also a biographical and descriptive note on each of his characters. It all amounted to a formidable pile of paper: nearly a thousand handwritten sheets for *Germinal*, about the same number for *La Terre*, and over twelve hundred for *La Débâcle*. Having in this way turned himself into something of an expert on each aspect of his subject, Zola was in a position to refute, quoting chapter and verse, the objections that seldom failed to be made by reviewers and correspondents who accused him of having distorted the facts and taken liberties with the truth. But the main purpose of all this laborious research and planning was to give him the self-confidence he needed to carry him through the purgatorial process of actually composing a new work.

The novels were, of course, much more than a digest of what Zola had learned about the way of life of actresses and playboys, of shop-assistants,

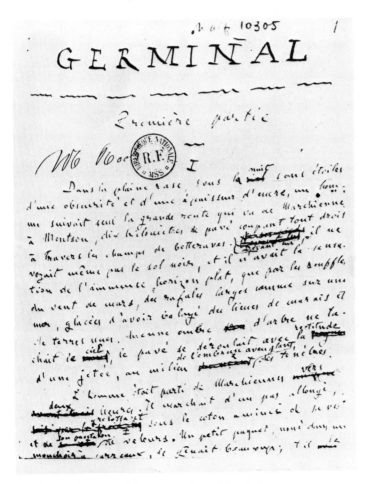

49 The opening page of the manuscript of *Germinal*

miners, farmers, railwaymen, stockbrokers. Since his invariable practice was to start by toying with the subject and working out the broad shape and direction the narrative was to take, the later stage of fact-finding was inevitably subordinate to certain aesthetic decisions already taken. His inquiries, however wide-ranging they might seem, were in fact carefully directed towards confirming or correcting points which he had previously assumed. Probably the best defence he ever put up for his use of documentation is embodied in an article he wrote for *Le Figaro* in 1896 on 'The Rights of the Novelist'. He argued here that the writer of fiction necessarily proceeds in a quite different way from the historian or the social scientist. 'All that can be asked of me is that I should start from the known facts, and establish firmly the ground on which I propose to stand; that is why I document myself, drawing on the indispensable sources. My proper function only begins thereafter; my real job is to create life with the elements which I have had to take where I found them. The one question to be asked is whether, having gathered together all the information currently available on a given subject, I have succeeded in selecting and binding up, like a strong-armed reaper, my sheaf of corn.'[5]

There is no doubt that, however exhaustive and objective the preliminary studies he made, when it actually came to the point of sitting down to write a new book, in front of that huge desk in his cluttered study at Médan, Zola wrought something specific, individualistic and inimitable. It may be supposed that, working independently with the same data as he had accumulated on the condition of the coal-mining industry in France in 1884, two trained social scientists could have produced, by and large, the same kind of report; neither of them would have written anything like *Germinal*. Zola was fond of quoting Flaubert, who used to say that one should research a subject thoroughly, but should have the courage, once one actually sat down to write the novel, to despise the knowledge previously amassed. What counted was not the blocks of masonry in themselves, but their disposition in the pillars, walls, towers and flying buttresses of the miraculous cathedral that the architect set himself to erect.

14 Zola and the Impressionists

We have already seen in an earlier chapter what close personal links were forged, in the years immediately preceding the outbreak of the Franco-Prussian War, between Zola and the group of artists later to be known as the Impressionists. He argued their case in a series of press campaigns, did his best to interpret their aims to an obtusely derisive public, and was looked on by the artists themselves as their principal spokesman and champion. But the calamitous events of 1870–1 destroyed this happy partnership by dispersing the group to the four winds. Cézanne, following Zola's own example, left the capital to avoid being trapped by the advancing Prussian armies and buried himself at L'Estaque for the duration. Renoir, drafted into the army, was stationed for a while at Bordeaux, where he may possibly have seen something of Zola. Manet stayed in Paris, enlisting in the National Guard as an artilleryman; Bazille was sent to the front. Pissarro fled first to Brittany and then crossed the Channel; a little later he was joined by Monet and the two refugees settled down temporarily on the outskirts of London to carry on with their work. The retreat Pissarro fixed on, a charmingly leafy suburb in Surrey, happened by an odd coincidence to be in the same parish where, many years later, Zola found a quiet refuge when the uproar caused by his intervention in the Dreyfus Affair obliged him to seek asylum in England.

Eventually, after peace was restored, the little knot of artists was able to reconstitute itself, though without Bazille, who had been killed in action. But for one reason or another, Zola no longer figured as their flag bearer to the same extent as he had in the pre-war period. Around 1866–8 it was still possible for him to believe that the main objective of his artist friends coincided with his own aesthetic of modernity. Instead of painting historical or mythological pictures or scenes set in exotic lands, as had Delacroix, Decamps and other artists of the romantic generation, they followed Courbet in choosing subjects drawn from contemporary life. Manet's *Olympia* was no reclining Venus, no oriental odalisque such as Ingres might have painted, but a commonplace slut that the artist had evidently picked off the street and painted just as he saw her; while the young men sitting on the grass in *Le Déjeuner sur l'herbe* were shown wearing the ordinary sloppy corduroy jackets normally sported for holiday outings. But in the post-war period, although the Impressionists continued to paint contemporary scenes, the subject itself came to count for less and less; what interested them chiefly was the way things looked under different daytime illumination, varying from the dazzling noonday glare of high summer to the weak and watery winter light refracted on snow-covered roads. They still concentrated exclusively on the external scene, and in that sense naturalism and impressionism could be regarded as twin movements; but they were more concerned with the fleeting effect than with the permanent reality, which meant that they needed to paint rapidly, neglecting precise details and leaving the contours of objects blurred. To Zola, as to most other art critics of the period, this made them seem slapdash, incapable of finishing a picture properly. His former admiration ebbed and his attitude shifted to incomprehension, impatience, disappointment and downright annoyance when he decided that not one of them, not even Manet, was fulfilling the promise they had seemed to hold forth when he espoused their cause so vehemently in 1866.

For a long time, however, these misgivings remained private, kept secret even from those closest to him. If his comments on the current art scene could no longer be read in the Paris newspapers, there was a good reason for this. Editors who remembered his blistering attack on the academicians in his first *Salon* and his eccentric defiance of all accepted canons of taste in his panegyric on Manet were understandably reluctant, in the atmosphere of stifling conformism that prevailed during the first seven years of the Third Republic, to allow him space in their columns to air his views. The consequence was that Zola found himself reduced to dispatching his accounts of the annual art exhibitions to the Marseilles newspaper *Le Sémaphore* and to Stassyulevitch in St Petersburg who had them translated into Russian and published in the *European Herald*. In Paris, these articles remained unread and unknown, and it was generally thought that Zola had retired from the fray and was no longer interested in defending his former friends.

Yet they were badly in need of defenders. None of them had achieved anything like the dramatic breakthrough into popular favour that the publication of *L'Assommoir* represented for Zola. None of them—not even Manet—was a recognized master, and yet that accolade was freely bestowed at the time on painters like Meissonier whose only gift lay in his dexterity in handling the paint-brush. Manet had, it is true, scored one great popular success: this was when his warm-toned portrait of a tubby beer-drinker, entitled *Le Bon Bock*, was exhibited at the 1873 *Salon*. But this picture, whatever its real merits, was appreciated by the mass of the public for reasons that had nothing to do with Manet's artistic intentions; its success was a fluke and was not repeated. As for the younger members of the group, most of whom depended on selling their pictures to make a livelihood, they struggled along in penury and neglect, buoyed up only by the conviction they all shared that their efforts were bound eventually to bring about the downfall of academicism and to usher in a new and more exciting phase in the history of French art.

In those days it was still the case, as it had been all through the nineteenth century, that no painter could be said to 'count' unless he

50 Manet's *Le Bon Bock*

exhibited regularly in the annual Paris *Salon*. But the advanced art that the Impressionists practised stood little chance of finding favour with the conservative judges who decided, each winter, which submissions should be granted the honour of being hung in the spring exhibition and which should be rejected. The verdicts they reached were just as wayward and unpredictable as they had been before the war; the year after winning popular and critical acclaim with his *Bon Bock*, Manet was mortified to learn that only one of the three new pictures he had sent in was pronounced acceptable. Realizing the hopelessness of their continued efforts to gatecrash the official *Salon*, a small group of *avant-garde* artists led by Monet and Pissarro decided that year to rent a gallery and open a private group exhibition. It was the first of the so-called independent exhibitions of which there were to be eight in all between 1874 and 1886.

The idea had first been mooted in the press by Paul Alexis, so that it seems likely Zola would have been kept informed about the new venture and would have gone along to view the exhibition when it opened in a studio loaned by Nadar. However, there are no records to tell us what he thought about it, nor whether he was more saddened than indignant at the almost universal ridicule that his friends' works aroused. He did, however, comment on the second independent exhibition, which was held the year after in Durand-Ruel's gallery in the Rue Lepeletier. At the end of a long and generally disparaging review of the official *Salon* which he sent to the *European Herald*, Zola appended a short section about this private show, devoting a few sentences to each of the principal exhibitors. In Monet, he singled out for praise 'the extraordinary *éclat* of his brush'. Berthe Morisot's seascapes showed 'an astonishing delicacy of execution'. Pissarro was described as 'an even starker revolutionary than Monet', and Renoir as 'a Rubens lit by the brilliant sun of Velazquez'.[1] Finally, Zola remarked on the peculiar fidelity with which Sisley rendered the snow-covered countryside in wintertime. The one painter in the group about whom he had serious reservations was Degas, who in spite of a fondness for contemporary low-life subjects which should have endeared him to Zola, did not appear to share the interest of the hard-core Impressionists in exploring the effects of sunlight out of doors.

The third of these private shows, and the first to be boldly entitled 'Exhibition of the Impressionists', was held in 1877, and once again Zola wrote a complimentary review, mentioning in particular Cézanne, who had not exhibited with the group the previous year. Thus his loyalty to his old friends remained unshaken through this difficult period when nearly every other art critic scoffed at the 'independent exhibitions', dismissing them contemptuously as a publicity stunt organized by a coterie of incompetents who thought that crankiness was a valid substitute for the talent they did not possess.

It was not until 1879–80 that certain underlying strains made themselves manifest in the long-standing solidarity between the Impressionists and their redoubtable champion. By this time, thanks to the sensational sales of *L'Assommoir* and *Nana*, Zola could regard himself as having 'arrived'; but where the Impressionists were concerned, the situation remained much as it had always been: no one could be persuaded to take them seriously. The occasional auctions at which their works were offered for sale realized derisory sums; and Zola drew his own conclusions from the fact that there were no buyers for their canvases, whereas there were hundreds of thousands of customers for his novels. When Monet applied to him for the occasional small loan, Zola gladly sent him the couple of hundred francs he needed; but in his heart of hearts he could not help measuring the distance he had come in the past ten or twelve years, and comparing the progress he had made in public esteem with the failure of Monet, Cézanne and Pissarro to make any real impact in their own sphere. Without conceding anything or abandoning any of his convictions, he had managed to impose himself; even if violently attacked, he already counted as one of the most prominent figures in the literary world. But in

51 The Café de la Nouvelle Athènes, a rendez-vous for the Impressionists in the 1870s

artistic circles his old friends, now moving into their forties, were still regarded as mere oddities. Could Zola be blamed if at this time he began to wonder whether, after all, they might not be *des ratés*, unfortunates who must be judged to have dropped out of the race for recognition and celebrity?

Sympathy arises from understanding, but understanding demands time and trouble. Zola simply could not spare the time needed to acquire understanding of what the Impressionists were doing. Absorbed by the sheer labour of turning out one long novel after another year in year out, planning it, researching it, writing it, and seeing it through the press, he had no leisure to listen to the painters discussing their discoveries as he used to in the 1860s. They had long since deserted the Café Guerbois and met now at the Café de la Nouvelle Athènes, in the Place Pigalle, at the top of the street where, the following century, Dr Jacques Emile-Zola lived in an apartment crammed with relics of his illustrious father's life and work. The Nouvelle Athènes, immortalized in Degas's *L'Absinthe*, was frequented not just by Manet, Degas and Renoir, but by a number of *avant-garde* critics and by at least two young friends of Zola, Paul Alexis and the Anglo-Irish writer George Moore; but it is not recorded that Zola ever set foot in the place.

He did, however, maintain occasional contact with the painters through his publisher Georges Charpentier who happened to be an enthusiastic and enlightened patron of the arts. Charpentier had a special liking for Renoir's style, which led him to commission a portrait of his wife and two small children; this picture, which Renoir exhibited at the 1879 *Salon*, was warmly praised even by the most hidebound critics. Cézanne,

52 Degas's *L'Absinthe* provides a view of the interior of the Café de la Nouvelle Athènes

introduced by Zola, was too shy a man to visit the Charpentiers very often, but Manet was regularly to be seen in their drawing-room. He and Zola were as close to one another then as they ever had been, and when Mme Zola expressed the wish to have her portrait done by Manet, as he had painted that of her husband years before, Manet was delighted to comply; the result is the pastel head now to be seen in the permanent Impressionist exhibition in Paris.

Manet had never belonged to the caucus of Impressionist artists who collectively organized the various independent exhibitions from 1874 onwards. One reason was that it had always been a rule among them that any artist who chose to send in his work for assessment by the *Salon* jury should not be allowed to participate in the independent exhibitions. This rule alone would have debarred Manet from joining up with the Impressionists, supposing he had wanted to. Moreover, by 1880 both

53 *Mme Charpentier and her children*, the picture of the publisher's family that established Renoir as a fashionable portrait painter

Renoir, who was now coming into prominence as a fashionable portrait-painter, and Monet, spurred by his friend's example and perhaps despairing of ever making his way as an independent, had made up their minds to compete for entry to the *Salon*. Thus it was left to Degas, Berthe Morisot and Pissarro to organize the fifth Impressionist exhibition that year. Fortunately they had two useful new recruits: Gauguin, then a young painter frequently to be seen at the Nouvelle Athènes, and Degas's American disciple Mary Cassatt. With the exception of Pissarro, all these artists were men and women with sufficient private means to scorn the recognized route to fame and fortune.

It is evidence of the gradual permeation of contemporary taste by Impressionism that in 1880 one at least of Monet's two entries, a riverside scene called *Lavacourt*, was accepted, as were both Renoir's submissions, the *Woman Gathering Mussels* and a *Sleeping Girl*. But all these pictures were hung where it was difficult to see them properly, and the two disappointed artists asked Cézanne to sound Zola out and see if he would come to their rescue by publishing a protest in *Le Voltaire*, the newspaper to which he was contributing a regular column at the time.

Zola evidently thought well of the idea. Although, as we have seen, he had been writing about the Impressionists, whenever occasion offered, all through the 1870s, every one of his articles had appeared abroad or in the provincial press; this was to be his first opportunity for over a decade to express his views on artistic developments in a widely read Paris newspaper. He accordingly wrote a series of no fewer than four long articles, in which he faithfully retraced the history of Impressionism and of the successive independent exhibitions. While sympathizing with the innovators' desire to break away from the stifling conventions of academic art, he could not altogether approve of their attempts to by-pass the jury by mounting private exhibitions; he insisted that the right thing to do was to continue battering at the doors of the Academy's sacred citadel, rather than set up camp outside, in a pointless gesture of defiance. By implication, therefore, Zola endorsed the decision by Renoir and Monet to submit their work to the adjudication of the jury, and deprecated the obstinacy of Degas and his followers who persisted in boycotting the *Salon*.

So far so good; but in what he had to say about the achievements to date of the Impressionist movement, Zola was noticeably more lukewarm than he had showed himself in his pre-war manifestoes in favour of Manet and the Batignolles group. He emphasized, rightly, the peculiar difficulties encountered by the artist who deserts his studio to try and paint in broad daylight. He drew attention to the exemplary importance of the newly discovered artists of Japan, suggesting, plausibly enough, that they had some share in encouraging the Impressionists to lighten their palette. But, in the last resort, honesty compelled him to admit that not one of the group had emerged as indisputably a master in the sense that David, Ingres and Delacroix had been masters in their own time. 'They are all precursors, the man of genius has not made his appearance. It is easy to see what they are aiming at, and one applauds their efforts; but one looks in vain for the masterpiece that is needed to impose the formula and make everyone do obeisance. That is why the Impressionists' campaign has not so far resulted in victory; they remain inadequate to the task they have undertaken, they are still stammering, incapable of finding the right word.' Even so, Zola concluded, although one can and must condemn them as 'incomplete, illogical, exaggerated, impotent', still, the future belongs to them, they are the 'true artisans of the age'.[2]

The Impressionists were not as hurt by Zola's frankness as one might have expected. Some of them may well have privately agreed with much of what he said. Cézanne in particular was deeply conscious of the gap between what he had achieved hitherto and what he saw as his ultimate goal. So the article series in *Le Voltaire* brought about no immediate rupture between Zola and his artist friends, and when Manet died in 1883 and the decision was taken by his executors to hold a posthumous exhibition of his works, it was thought perfectly natural that Zola should write the introduction to the catalogue.

The event that ultimately set Zola at loggerheads with the Impressionists was the publication in 1886 of his novel *L'Œuvre*, the hero of which, Claude Lantier, is depicted as a gifted artist who gathers around him a group of disciples, but can never succeed in painting the 'masterpiece', the picture that will establish him for all time as a man of true genius. In the end he hangs himself in despair in front of his still unfinished canvas. In the passages of the book that tell of Claude's earlier life, Zola was obviously recalling Cézanne's youth; Claude's relations with his model and mistress Christine Hallegrain are closely similar to Cézanne's with Hortense Fiquet, and the friendship between Claude and the novelist Pierre Sandoz clearly mirrors that which existed between Cézanne and Zola himself. On the other hand Claude, in the novel, is looked up to by the other revolutionary painters as their leader; at no stage had Cézanne been regarded as heading the Impressionist movement. Rather, this role had devolved on Monet, and most of Claude's paintings that Zola describes in *L'Œuvre* can be equated with works signed by Monet, except for the first, which is suspiciously like Manet's *Déjeuner sur l'herbe* and is greeted, in the novel, with the same irreverent ridicule on the part of the viewers as they had heaped on Manet's masterpiece when it was first shown at the *Salon des Refusés* in 1863.

It is clear, then, that the central character in *L'Œuvre*, presented as a man stumbling along the frontier that divides genius from madness, was a composite figure in whom none the less Cézanne—the painter whom Zola personally knew best—is recognizable as the principal model. Little wonder then that, having read his complimentary copy of the book, Cézanne should have sent the author a curt note of thanks and thereafter, for the rest of Zola's life, studiously avoided meeting him. The other members of the group were almost as indignant. It seemed to them all too obvious that, under the cover of fiction, Zola had presented the Impressionists as being, individually and collectively, sad failures. They realized, rightly, that they could no longer count on him to champion them, and from that point on they ceased to have any further dealings with him.

15 Jeanne

Directly he had finished *L'Œuvre*, Zola turned with relief to a long-cherished project, his 'study of peasant life'. With his keen sense of the value of newspaper publicity, Zola was always very ready to talk to journalists about his future plans, and in the references he made in these interviews to the forthcoming *La Terre* he always stressed the pleasure he expected to derive from writing it, calling it his 'favourite book',[1] 'the novel he had set his heart on'.[2] This is understandable, for his feelings for the countryside ran very deep. His happiest memories of boyhood were connected with long country rambles. His grandparents on his mother's side, whom he remembered with such affection, were true country people, natives of that fertile plain of the Beauce which he ultimately chose as the setting for *La Terre*. Though himself a Parisian by birth, Zola never really took to city life. As a young man living and working in the capital, he seized every opportunity to escape from it on Sunday outings to the nearby woods and riverside holidays at Bennecourt. The first wish he gratified, as soon as he found himself with a few spare thousand-franc notes, was to purchase a house and grounds in the country.

Médan was a real village, not a suburb of Paris. Though he lived there only half the year, Zola took the trouble to make friends with the local farmers, served on the parish council and listened with interest to the village gossip relayed to him by his own domestic staff. But for his novel he wanted a more isolated setting, somewhere in the deep heart of rural France.

With the faithful Alexandrine at his side, he set out in search of it on 3 May 1886. They travelled down to Chartres by train and from there drove to Châteaudun in a hired horse-drawn landau. After a visit to the cattle market they pushed on further south, to Cloyes. On the 8th Zola was shown over two or three big farms in the neighbourhood and at one of them saw the sheep being sheared. But that was all: he was back in Médan on the 11th. The expedition was much briefer than he had envisaged at an earlier stage, when he talked of spending a whole month on a farm, pretending his doctor had recommended the benefits of country air; he had planned to take his meals with the farmer and his family, wander round the fields watching the ploughmen at work, listen to the villagers talking of an evening. His impatience to get started made him abandon this idyllic project. He began writing the book in June 1886, but progress was slow; his subject was so vast, he complained, and the tasks of compression and selection had never posed so many problems. By March

54 Manet's pastel portrait of Alexandrine Zola, executed in 1879

the following year *La Terre* was still only two-thirds written, and he was being chivvied by the editor of *Le Gil Blas* who had booked the serial rights. To pacify him, Zola agreed that *La Terre* should begin appearing in the newspaper on 29 May 1887, even though the complete text was far from ready. From then on it was a race to write the remaining chapters before the relentless succession of instalments caught up with him. Tired out, badly in need of a holiday, Zola finished the book on 18 August.

On the very same day, by what can only have been a malign coincidence, there appeared in *Le Figaro* a lengthy denunciation of his book signed by five young novelists; this was the document that has gone down in history as the 'Manifesto of the Five against *La Terre*'. None of the signatories belonged to Zola's inner circle of acquaintances, and if they had met him at all this could only have been at Champrosay, where Alphonse Daudet lived, or else at Edmond de Goncourt's place at Auteuil. It is indeed only too likely that the idea of writing this scurrilous and unprovoked attack, if it did not actually emanate from one or other of these treacherous friends, was secretly fostered by them.

The general drift of the Manifesto was that Zola, having struck so brave a blow for the cause of truthfulness in literature when he published *L'Assommoir*, had since then not just deserted the cause but brought the gravest discredit on it. The novels he had gone on to write after *L'Assommoir* were informed less and less by a genuine desire to present reality as he saw it, and more and more by 'a violent bias towards obscenity'; a trend which might, the writers speculated, have originated in the base calculation that the profits of pornography were greater than those earned by serious literature, or which might equally well be due to some 'affection of the writer's lower organs, the nasty habits of a solitary monk'[3] which inclined him to dwell on filth and lechery in his fictional writing.

With shameless indelicacy, the authors of the manifesto developed this theme, arguing that Zola's well-known sexual continence reflected little credit on him since it was a virtue born of necessity. 'In his youth he was very poor and very timid, and woman, whom he never knew at the age one should, haunts him now in the shape of a palpably unreal vision. Then there is the disequilibrium due to his kidney complaint, which no doubt causes him to be needlessly preoccupied with certain physical functions ... To these different sources of his morbid condition one should perhaps add an anxiety, so often observed among misogynists as also among adolescent boys, concerning his sexual competence.'[4]

In public, Zola affected to treat this libellous attack—a kick in the balls if there ever was one—with the contempt it deserved. In the course of a stormy career he had had plenty of practice in digesting insults, though they had never before descended to this level of indecent innuendo. For some years he had amused himself cutting out and filing away every derogatory article that had appeared in print about him, with the idea that he might one day reprint the best or the worst of them in a book to be called *Leurs Injures*—a title clearly intended to hark back to that of his first volume of criticism, *Mes Haines*. It was not the case that he shrugged off abuse with Olympian indifference; by his own account he positively revelled in it, and when his eye was caught by some piece of angry invective in the morning paper he would put it aside in order to read and savour it at leisure in the evening. After all, 'the greatest men are those who are most savagely attacked, and as soon as the attacks die down, that constitutes proof that they are on the decline'.[5]

Besides, it would be surprising if Zola had not anticipated and discounted in advance some protest about the immorality of his new novel. *La Terre*, which for most critics today ranks with *L'Assommoir* and *Germinal* as one of the three summits of his literary achievement, is structured on an antithesis between the bounteous serenity of Nature and the fretful, sordid greed of the men and women who hang on her like the hideous parasites they are. Zola used every device at his disposal to bring out the contrast between the beauty of the countryside and the vileness of the country dwellers, whom he presents in the mass as a plague of noisome insects and individually as 'lubricious gorillas'. In addition, *La Terre* was deliberately intended to correct the idyllic picture of pastoral innocence that earlier writers of rustic novels, George Sand first and foremost, had popularized. The peasants of Rognes are sly, callous, brutal, avaricious, but above all libidinous, treacherously and tirelessly so. In no other of his books does Zola accumulate so many scenes of goatish copulation, frustrated rape, actual rape, incest and sadistic murder. *La Terre* is more shocking than *Nana* because the 'poem of man's sexual desire' has lost all its fire and glamour; the characters, in spite of Jean Macquart's real but unappreciated tenderness for Françoise, are in general simply human animals in rut.

But even though he must have been prepared for some expressions of indignation on the part of outraged sentimentalists and purple-faced prudes, he could hardly have anticipated that criticism would take the defamatory form it did in the 'Manifesto of the Five'. The passage we have quoted forms only a small portion of the complete diatribe, which was as wordy as it was priggish, but it is likely that, however little he may have been affected by the rest of the philippic—in attacking him as a venal pornographer these young men were not, after all, saying anything that had not been said several times before—the reference to his sexual timidity, to his enforced continence, and to the 'nasty habits of solitary monks' pierced even his shell of indifference. For, like all smears, it did embody a vestige of the truth. Zola knew himself to have been, all his life, unadventurous where women were concerned. He knew how much of what he had suppressed, in the way of desires and longings, had found compensatory outlet in the erotic scenes he had written into almost every one of his novels. He had been Laurent tumbling Thérèse Raquin on an adulterous bed, Maxime embracing his wanton stepmother in *La Curée*, Serge eating the forbidden fruit with Albine in *La Faute de l'abbé Mouret*, Muffat submitting masochistically to Nana's brutal whims, and Claude Lantier, in *L'Œuvre*, feasting his eyes on Christine's firm young breasts as she lay quietly sleeping. Every morning, alone in his study, he had caressed all these unreal phantoms, so real to him, blonde, dark-haired, shy, passionate, promiscuous or innocent; and every night he had lain alongside the same woman, who had certainly been beautiful when he first knew her but who was now in her late forties, growing stout and for ever complaining of her poor health. Was he condemned for all time to use his pen to cheat his senses?

Except for a short period in the first weeks of his exile in England, Zola never kept a diary. His letters—other than those he wrote around the age of twenty—are mostly brief, business-like, unintimate communications, quite unlike the self-revealing letters Flaubert wrote to his friends. But among his papers one does find just a few texts where his inmost thoughts were put down purely for the private record with no thought that his words might be read by anyone else; the very rarity of such texts enhances their value as testimony. One of them is embodied in the draft plan of *Le Rêve*, the novel that followed *La Terre*.

Zola had no idea, when he started work on it, what *Le Rêve* was to be about, but he had a clear picture of the kind of novel he wanted it to be: something tranquil and innocent, forming a complete contrast with *La Terre*. It would be a book such as nobody would expect him to write, or would suppose him capable of writing, with qualities of purity and spirituality which would confound all his critics. He would find room in it, he hoped, for the transcendental, the unknowable, the dream world: hence the title.

The first idea he tried out was to have at the centre of the story 'a man of forty, ignorant of love, having devoted himself entirely to science up till then, who is seized with a passion for a girl of sixteen. She would be in love with him, or imagine she was: the whole story of her awakening; then falling for a young man, a relative of the forty-year-old, youth calling to youth. The sufferings of the older man, and in the end he yields, he gives the girl up to the young man.' Such a scenario, Zola goes on to say, would fulfil most of the conditions he wanted to observe in his new novel, except for the irrational element, the presence of the dream world. How about letting the older man be professionally engaged in research into spiritualism, hypnotism, or parapsychology, 'some branch of science still in its infancy, with the thrilling sense of penetrating the darkness of a mystery'? Zola let his mind play with this possibility, which obviously made a strong appeal to him. 'That would be fine, symbolic, showing him at first seeking to discover the unknown, letting his own youth slip by, forgetting about love in his pursuit of a will-o'-the-wisp. (Myself, my own work, literature which has devoured my life, then the turmoil, the crisis, the need to find love, all that to be studied in its psychological aspect.)'[9] His scientist would wake up to the fact that his lifetime of study had been the dream, and that the girl represented reality. 'At the end of his researches, there is still only woman, this is what he confesses to himself. His tears as he realizes he has wasted his life, old age at hand when love will no longer be possible, the body failing.'[6]

In the end Zola rejected this plot, or at least modified it in such a way that the element of personal confession was eliminated. But the manuscript text, moving in its directness and evident sincerity, remains as a testimony to Zola's state of mind immediately before he met Jeanne Rozerot, the girl he was to fall in love with, who was to fall in love with him, and with whom he was to experience perhaps the greatest joys life ever brought him but also anxieties and terrors of a kind spared him hitherto in his busy but fairly humdrum existence. The words put in parenthesis show that he was ready for such an adventure, and explain

55 The Zolas' house at Médan

why: the sense of having missed out on a passionate love affair in the course of a lifetime's struggle to achieve his literary ambitions; together with the apprehension that, as the years fled past, he would soon be too old to enjoy the sweetness of a young girl's embraces.

And in any case what chance had he of attracting any woman's attention, let alone that of a virginal sixteen-year-old, with his sweaty round face and paunchy body? In 1887 Zola measured 44 inches round what used to be his waist and tipped the scales at 212 lb. Twelve years earlier, in an attempt to rid himself of his chronic nervous trembling, he had given up smoking and ever since had put on weight steadily until now, as he sat there trying to plan his next novel in the sad grey light of a November morning, with his pet dog snoring on a sofa in the corner of the room, he felt it as altogether grotesque that he should be allowing himself to indulge in so impossible a *dream*. He had arranged to spend that evening at the theatre: Antoine was producing a new play by his disciple Léon Hennique. At the end of the interval, sauntering back to his box along one of the corridors of the Théâtre Libre, he found himself face to face with the painter Raffaëlli and pressed himself against the wall to let the other man pass; the passage was narrow, and Zola muttered his excuses: 'Such a nuisance to have a corporation like mine!' As he slid past, Raffaëlli turned and said: 'You know, if you want a very simple way of slimming, all you need do is not to drink with your meals.'[7] Then he hurried off, but his words stayed in Zola's mind and at lunch the next day he told the maid to take away his wineglass. Mme Zola laughed and said

56 A caricature by Raffaëlli of Zola before he started to slim; Manet is seated beside him

he would never be able to keep it up; but she was forgetting the dogged persistence he could display when he set his mind to something, and in any case she was not in the secret of her husband's private motives for wanting to slim.

Combined with complete abstinence from starchy foods, bread in particular, the new diet worked wonders. In three months Zola lost 30 lb. Edmond de Goncourt, who had kept out of his way since the publication of the 'Manifesto of the Five', was astonished when he met him again at a dinner-party given by Charpentier to get his two quarrelsome authors to bury the hatchet. 'It's positively true,' he noted in his diary that night, 'his stomach has melted away and his personality has, as it were, become fine-drawn and taut, and what is particularly curious is that the delicately moulded features he used to have in the past, which were all lost and buried in the round fat face he had acquired in the last few years, have reappeared, so that he is really beginning to look once more like Manet's portrait, but with a hint of wickedness in his expression.'[8]

The following summer, having finished writing *Le Rêve*, Zola left with his wife to take a six weeks' break at Royan, on the mouth of the Gironde. The pretext for these summer excursions away from Médan, which the couple had taken most years since 1875, was always Mme Zola's state of health. In 1884 and 1885 they had stayed at a mountain spa, but after that they had taken to spending the hot season at Royan or the nearby seaside village of Saint Palais. The Charpentiers owned some property down there, and Alexandrine's cousins, the Laborde family, had their home near by. Normally Zola would take down whatever work he was engaged on, but in 1888 he decided to make it a proper holiday and to the delight and amazement of Charpentier and his lively friend the engraver Fernand Desmoulin, joined them in all their boating and fishing expeditions. An additional member of the little group was the mayor of Royan, Billaud, whose hobby was photography, and Zola spent hours in his makeshift laboratory being initiated into the mysteries of gelatine emulsions, bromide prints, the collodion wet-plate process, and the very latest thing, celluloid roll film. Zola purchased one of the 'Kodaks' put on the market for the first time that year and began experimenting on his own account, with quite remarkable results from the start.

Among those he asked to pose for him was a good-looking twenty-year-old girl whom his wife had engaged the previous May to help with the mending and sewing. He took a charming picture of her sitting in the garden threading a needle in front of an overflowing work-table, and

57 Zola and his new hobby; examining negatives

another where she is shown walking along a rutted country road, her face shaded under a wide-brimmed hat and a parasol. Mme Zola, who preferred to stay indoors in the afternoon heat, was only too thankful that her husband had found himself an alternative companion for his strolls. That his interest in Jeanne might take a dangerous turn was a possibility that never crossed her mind, lulled as she was into a false security by twenty-two years of constant affection and irreproachable fidelity. Besides, he wasn't a lady's man, poor Emile, anything but . . .

Jeanne-Sophie-Adèle Rozerot was the daughter of a miller living in Burgundy. She had no real memory of her mother, having lost her when she was only two; her father had remarried and started another family. When this happened, she and her older sister were given a new home by her dead mother's parents. She had gone into service as soon as she was of age to do so and was, to all intents and purposes, alone in the world.

It did not take Zola long to learn her brief and rather sad history. Her quiet voice, the cool fragrance of her skin in the warm September sunshine, her long black hair and full red lips, which reminded him vaguely of his boyhood passion, Louise Solari, dead now so many years ago, all this moved him strangely. Was this not just what he had hoped for, dismissing the hope as sheer madness? For his dream to become reality, he had only to speak. The tremor in his voice when he did so seemed to the girl some guarantee of the sincerity of the words he used. Besides, his approach was more that of a respectful suitor than a self-confident seducer. All he asked was that they should keep in touch after the summer was over. He did not want her to go back to Médan, as one of the staff; nor could there be any question of her taking a position in some other household. He begged her to let him find her a pretty little apartment in a quiet part of Paris where he could visit her and where they could get to know one another better.

Jeanne found it impossible to refuse this offer, made with such discretion and solicitude. The flat that he took for her when they left Royan in October was situated in the Rue St Lazare, a stone's throw from the big railway station that he knew he would be having to visit fairly frequently to document himself for his next novel, *La Bête humaine*. If a reporter or any of his casual acquaintances saw him in the district, the assumption would be that the novelist was going about his normal business, for everyone knew that railways were to be the subject of the seventeenth volume of the *Rougon-Macquart* series. He was able to call most afternoons; they would drink tea together in the lace-curtained sitting-room; and after a couple of months of this gentle courtship, one day in December 1888 when the evening shadows fell early, Jeanne gave herself to him trustingly and unregretfully.

58 *Opposite* Jeanne sewing in the garden at Royan, as photographed by Zola

16 A Double Life

Zola's mind was now in a greater turmoil than it had been the previous summer in Royan. For the first time in his life he had a secret—a secret which he had to keep, for he had no illusions about the way it would affect his wife if it came to her knowledge, but which he was longing none the less to pour into a sympathetic ear. Edmond de Goncourt was interested that, for once, Zola nodded in agreement when he started talking about how they and all their generation had been 'true martyrs to literature', in the sense that they had devoted the whole of their lives to authorship and in the process had forgotten to live. But he was even more surprised to hear Zola pick up the theme and enlarge on it, admitting that in recent months he found himself seized by a new yearning to enjoy the pleasures he had denied himself for so long; gripping the older man by the elbow, he pointed out of the window murmuring: 'Yes, I can't see a girl like that walk past without asking myself: "Doesn't that count for more than a book?" '[1] This was in January 1889; in March he made another veiled confession, explaining to Huysmans why *La Bête humaine* was coming along so slowly. The unavowable reason was that he was spending every spare hour he dared with Jeanne; but he talked to Huysmans about his 'suppressed laziness' which was rising to the surface and added: 'It's a mood of indifference, when I keep asking myself: "What's the point?" I am following its progress in myself with curiosity.'[2]

La Bête humaine, planned and written entirely in the first year of his liaison, betrays his state of mind in an interestingly oblique fashion. It is at once the grimmest, most pessimistic and, in parts, most torridly erotic of his works, but what, with hindsight, one can see as most revealing is the way Zola conceived each of the major characters in the novel as hugging to his bosom some guilty secret, which has at all costs to be kept hidden from the others. The first secret is sprung in an opening chapter of unexampled violence, when Roubaud discovers that his young wife Séverine has had an affair with a senile millionaire, Grandmorin, one of the directors of the railway company for which he works. He drags the details out of her with kicks and blows, and then forces her to write the old man a letter of assignation that draws him to his death. Roubaud commits the murder, having compelled Séverine to assist him, in the carriage of an express train; the scene is glimpsed very briefly by Jacques Lantier, who happens to be standing near the line when the train flashes past: another secret surprised. Partly to ensure his silence at the judicial inquiry, Séverine makes approaches to the young man and eventually becomes his

59 Jeanne walking down a country road, photographed by Zola. The landscape, the strong sunlight, and the parasol motif give this photograph a distinct affinity with an Impressionist canvas

mistress. The secret of their liaison has of course to be kept from Roubaud, but is guessed by Flore, the daughter of a level-crossing keeper, who nurtures a hidden passion for Jacques. In an attempt to revenge herself, she brings about a derailment of the train in which Séverine is a passenger. Both Jacques and Séverine survive the accident, and Flore kills herself. Then Séverine tries to persuade her lover to murder Roubaud, but Jacques has his own terrible secret: he knows himself to be subject to uncontrollable fits of homicidal mania during which he finds himself driven to seek sexual satisfaction by stabbing to death any woman he happens to be with. Séverine herself is eventually an uncomprehending victim of one of these murderous rages. The whole of *La Bête humaine* can be deciphered as a cryptogram in which the underlying message is repeated again and again: I am guilty, I must keep my guilt secret, there is nothing to be feared more than discovery, the catastrophe that would overwhelm me in that event is too terrible to contemplate . . .

60 Illustration for the opening chapter of *La Bête humaine*

Zola's state of anxiety was, if anything, exacerbated when it was discovered that Jeanne was pregnant. Alexandrine's childlessness was something which had never greatly troubled Zola but which, as the years passed by, she herself felt as a shameful stigma. His brain reeled at the thought of the violence of her reactions if it should ever come to her ears that her husband had not simply taken a young mistress but was founding a family with her. But when, only a little more than nine months after they became lovers, Jeanne gave birth to a little girl, his feelings changed again. Was it not a true pledge, guaranteeing their future together? Denise in the cradle made their union unbreakable. And besides, the thought of this unexpected fatherhood gave him a new sense of power, released in him sources of confident energy which he thought had run quite dry. 'I am passing through a very sound period where my work is concerned,' he wrote to Charpentier. 'I am in an excellent state of health, I feel once more as I did when I was twenty, ready to devour mountains.'[3]

This letter was written just three weeks before the expected date of Jeanne's confinement. Zola had used, as a pretext for not joining the Charpentiers at Royan that year, the excuse that he needed to put the finishing touch to *La Bête humaine* at Médan, with all his documents around him.

But even after the baby was born, he remained torn and troubled. Granted Alexandrine had grown stout, acidulous and apt to grumble about imaginary ailments, but he could never forget the past, those spring mornings in the Bois de Verrières, the years of worry and poverty they had struggled through together side by side, and then when at last the money started to flow in, the pleasure they had taken in acquiring and furnishing the house at Médan. She had surrounded him with the quiet he needed for his work, she had been the ideal secretary, filing away his papers and making sure none of them went astray; he remembered, affectionately, the scene she had made when he admitted having promised Jules Laffitte he could have the manuscript of *Nana* as a present. (They said that Laffitte had sold it, later on, to some rich American, Morgan, wasn't that his name? Yes, Pierpont Morgan, who had paid him some outrageous sum, twelve thousand francs or more.) And then again, she had always been so welcoming to his friends, even those she couldn't stand, like poor Cézanne. He had every reason to be grateful to her, and yet what he was doing now was, he knew for a certainty, the one thing that would cut her to the heart if ever she came to know about it.

So it had to be kept from her, but as time went on he found it more and more difficult to make a mystery of his new-found happiness. The first friend he confided in was, predictably, the closest friend he had, the one who would never see wrong in anything he did: Paul Alexis. Paul's wife Marie agreed to stand godmother to the little Denise, and it fell to Alexis to act as message-bearer when anything occurred to prevent Zola from visiting Jeanne. Unfortunately Alexis was not as discreet as he should have been and the news was soon all over Paris. Some were envious, some amused, others pretended to be indignant; but at least there was no more talk of the 'solitary monk'; the uglier charges in the 'Manifesto of the Five' had been totally refuted.

In 1891 Jeanne found herself pregnant again. Vaguely remorseful, feeling he ought to do something to compensate for the wrongs he was inflicting on Alexandrine, Zola set off twice that year on long expeditions with her. In April they toured the battlefields of the eastern front, ostensibly so that Zola could document himself for his forthcoming war-novel, *La Débâcle*. Then, in September, as if unable in his nervousness to settle anywhere, or else fearful that some rumour might reach her if they stayed at home, he interrupted his work on the book to take her away on a trip down to the Pyrenees. This meant that he could not be at hand when his second child was born; but Céard had agreed to help Jeanne when her time came and to let him have the news by means of a prearranged code advertisement in *Le Figaro*; and this was how he learned of the birth of his son, Jacques, on 25 September.

It was to Céard too that he turned when the inevitable happened at last: Mme Zola, alerted by an anonymous 'well-wisher', searched her husband's study and broke open the box in which he kept all Jeanne's letters. On 11 November 1891 Céard received a telegram: 'My wife is going mad. Can you go to the Rue St Lazare and take the necessary steps? Forgive me.' Céard knew exactly what this meant: Jeanne, the two-year-old Denise and the six-week-old Jacques had to be taken to a place of safety before Alexandrine could get to their apartment. The next few weeks were horrible. Zola had said his wife was going mad and it really seemed as though she were; had she found her young rival when she burst into the Rue St Lazare establishment, she might well have carried out her threat to murder not just the mother but the two small children as well. Zola found it useless to try and reason with her; the servants were terrorized and he had to have their bedroom padded to deaden the sound of her screaming.

Céard, whose sympathies inclined more to the wife than to the husband in this crisis, suggested divorce as the one sensible solution. But divorce had been legalized in France for less than ten years and was still regarded as a desperate remedy. Sobered momentarily, Alexandrine began to think what her social position would be if the rupture between her and her husband were publicly admitted. In what houses would she continue to be received? Humiliating as the role of the betrayed wife might be, anything was preferable to the equivocal status of an ageing *divorcée*. Useless, too, to exact a promise from Emile that he should cease seeing his concubine and her bastard brood; even if he gave it, he would break it.

By the beginning of August 1892 Céard was able to tell his mother, who was proposing to visit the Zolas, that she would find things a lot quieter, though he feared it was only a temporary lull and that a more permanent solution would have to be found sooner or later. He was wrong about this. Yielding first one position, then another, Mme Zola finally accepted the situation as the price that had to be paid for preserving appearances. She accompanied her husband on another long trip to the south later that month; it was one way of demonstrating to their friends, among whom the wildest rumours had been circulating, that they were still a united couple, or at least intended so to conduct themselves in the eyes of the world. On their return Zola installed Jeanne and the children in a small rented house at Cheverchemont, a hamlet a mile or so distant from Médan, where Alexis and his wife were living. Apart from Céard, these two were practically the only friends Jeanne had. Cheverchemont was near enough for Zola to bicycle over in the afternoon—Jeanne and he were both keen cyclists, and so too was Marie Alexis, though her husband never managed to keep his balance for more than a few turns of the pedals. On clear mornings, looking through a pair of field-glasses from his study window at the top of the house, Zola was able to watch Denise and Jacques playing in the garden, minute figures on a distant lawn.

Alexandrine was not unaware of the purpose of these comings and goings, but felt a little grateful to Emile for having the decency to make a mystery of them. She nerved herself to get her husband to talk about the children and eventually, one afternoon, she asked him to bring them to the house. From then on she took an increasing interest in Denise and Jacques and when she was away from home, in the long, tenderly affectionate, daily letters that Zola sent her, after giving her news about any visitors who had called, about the latest meeting of the Société des Gens de Lettres and his progress on the current novel, he always included a bulletin about the children. 'I went over Denise's homework with her [the little girl was then just six] and tested her on her scripture lesson. You can't imagine her way of telling the story of Isaac's wedding and Joseph sold into slavery by his brothers, with such conviction in her voice and gestures. Jacques has heard the same lessons repeated so often that he knows them too, and you ought to hear him rolling his tongue round the names Canaan, Mesopotamia . . .'[4] It is hard to decide which is stranger: that Zola should have kept his lawful wife informed about the activities of his children by another woman, or that this obdurate freethinker should have displayed such solicitude for their religious education. In a novel he would never have permitted himself such paradoxes; but then facts have rarely the logic of fiction.

61 A passing locomotive photographed by Zola at Médan

17 London, Lourdes and Rome

The double life that Zola was leading in these years, full of remorse and anxiety, but also of moments of the purest joy, coincided with the zenith of his fame as a writer. With *Le Docteur Pascal*, which is in part a glamorized transposition of his autumnal love affair, the twenty-volume *Rougon-Macquart* cycle was at last completed, and his publishers decided to mark the occasion with a banquet held in a fashionable restaurant in the Bois de Boulogne. It is evidence of the jealousy and ill-will that beset Zola, despite or because of his unique position in the world of letters, that none of his most eminent fellow novelists could be prevailed on to deliver the congratulatory speech at the end of the dinner—neither Edmond de Goncourt, nor Alphonse Daudet, nor Joris-Karl Huysmans; Maupassant was at the time dying wretchedly in an asylum for the insane. In the end they had to ask Catulle Mendès, a minor Parnassian poet and fervent Wagnerian, whose only real connection with Zola was that he had agreed to publish the later instalments of *L'Assommoir* in his magazine, *La République des Lettres*, when the editor of the newspaper that had started serializing it refused to continue.

The seal on his international celebrity was set later the same year (1893) when he was invited to visit London as the guest of the Institute of Journalists. When the letter arrived, Zola was in a quandary whether to accept or civilly decline the honour. Of all the countries in the world where his novels were read (and by this time they were numerous: *La Débâcle*, on its appearance, was translated immediately into English, German, Spanish, Italian, Portuguese, Russian, Czech, Danish, Dutch, Norwegian and Swedish), Great Britain was the one where critical hostility had been the fiercest. The first, carefully bowdlerized translations appeared in 1884, the rights having been negotiated with Zola by George Moore on behalf of Vizetelly & Co. This firm had been established by Henry Vizetelly, the father of the journalist Ernest Alfred Vizetelly whose name we have come across already, and specialized in translations of the major French and Russian writers of the mid nineteenth century, Flaubert, Daudet, Tolstoy and Dostoyevsky. Henry Vizetelly was persuaded to add Zola to his list when an American translation of *Nana* became a best-seller in the United States.

Scandalized comment was rife from the start, but it was only when he issued a version—much watered down even so—of *La Terre* that Vizetelly ran into serious trouble. A vindictive campaign, spearheaded by the National Vigilance Association, was launched against the hapless bookseller and in

62 Zola's two children, Denise and Jacques, whom he has photographed here blowing bubbles

the House of Commons Samuel Smith, M.P. for Flintshire, introduced a motion deploring 'the rapid spread of demoralizing literature in this country'. In a virulent speech he attacked Zola by name and said of his works that 'nothing more diabolical had ever been written by the pen of man; they were only fit for swine, and those who read them must turn their minds into cesspools.'[1] Although the Home Secretary, replying to the debate, agreed that contemporary French literature appeared to be 'written with the object of directing attention to the foulest passions of which human nature was capable'[2] and ought therefore to be left in the decent obscurity of a foreign language, he expressed some doubts about the propriety of asking the Public Prosecutor to take proceedings against Zola's English publisher; such action had better be left to private initiative.

It was not long in coming. Within weeks Henry Vizetelly was summoned to answer the charge of publishing three obscene libels (trans-

63 Zola and his wife posing with a group of top-hatted Victorians in front of the Savoy Hotel, London

lations of *Nana* and *Pot-Bouille* besides *La Terre*) and was so terrorized by the invective directed against him, in manifest contempt of the *sub judice* rules, by an unholy alliance of politicians, preachers and leader-writers that he abstained from putting up any defence. He was fined £100 and bound over for twelve months. Before this term was up, he was sent for trial again in respect of his translations of other works by Zola and also of Maupassant's *Bel-Ami* and Bourget's *Crime d'amour*. This time the sixty-nine-year-old publisher was given a stiff prison sentence and the firm he had founded was forced into liquidation.

These events had taken place as recently as 1888–9, and it is understandable, therefore, that Zola should have felt serious misgivings about the wisdom of paying an official visit to a country whose legislative chamber and law courts had so recently pronounced him a pornographer. He expressed these doubts to the two English journalists he was in contact with, E. A. Vizetelly and R. H. Sherard, and only when both of them urged him to make the journey, if only to demonstrate the absurdity of current British prejudices about him, did he dispatch his acceptance.

As it turned out, the advice he was given proved sound and he had no cause to regret having acted on it. A powerful backlash against the stuffier manifestations of the non-conformist conscience had already set in, and as soon as he arrived on these shores Zola found himself treated almost as though he were a national hero. Alighting from his train at the London terminal, he was greeted by Sir Edward Levy-Lawson, editor of the *Daily Telegraph*, who read an address of welcome in French, after which he and his wife were driven to the Savoy Hotel. The paper he read to the Institute, which as we have seen he took so much trouble to get by heart, was listened to politely by an international audience of journalists assembled at Lincoln Inn Hall; the subject, anonymity in the press, was innocuous enough. There was a banquet at the Crystal Palace, followed by a firework display in the course of which, as he told Jeanne in one of his hastily scribbled letters, his own portrait appeared as one of the set pieces. He attended a reception at the Imperial Institute and a ball at the Guildhall at which the Lord Mayor was host and where, as Jeanne was again informed, the four thousand guests stood and clapped him on his arrival. Time was also found for some ritual sightseeing. The Zolas were taken to view Greenwich Observatory and were shown round the National Gallery and Westminster Abbey. He was greatly impressed by the arrangements made for readers at the Library of the British Museum, which he was kind enough to say were much superior to anything at the Bibliothèque Nationale. Vizetelly thought it might be interesting for the author of *L'Assommoir* to visit the East End, but after their exploration of the back-alleys of Whitechapel, still reeking with the blood shed by Jack the Ripper, Zola told him that as far as he could judge, the slums of London were nowhere near as bad as those he had seen in Paris. Clearly he had little to learn of the arts of diplomacy.

The five-week visit was rounded off by a dinner at the Authors' Club at which Zola found he had to reply to a toast. The tenor of his speech showed that the overwhelming cordiality of his welcome had not gone to his head. 'Amidst all the plaudits, I well understand that the opinion of your critics has not changed in regard to my works. Only you have seen the author, and found him less black than report painted him. . . . Works of a different order in art to your own may have affronted you, but you were too sensible to refrain from according them some recognition as soon as you understood how much effort and sincerity they embodied.'[3] Zola concluded with the ritual formula: 'Here I say good-bye, or rather *au revoir.*' Neither he, nor any of those present, could possibly have imagined under what totally different circumstances he was to see London again before the decade was out.

The following year (1894) he made another journey abroad, this time to Rome. His visit was, however, undertaken for quite different reasons, and

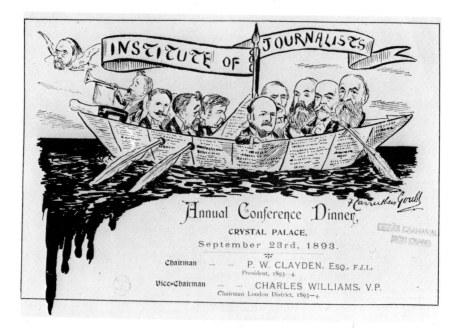

INSTITUTE OF JOURNALISTS

Annual Conference Dinner,

CRYSTAL PALACE,

September 23rd, 1893.

Chairman	... ...	P. W. CLAYDEN, ESQ., F.J.I., President, 1893—4.
Vice=Chairman	... ...	CHARLES WILLIAMS, V.P. Chairman London District, 1893—4.

64 Invitation card to the Crystal Palace banquet. Zola is represented, rather incongruously (top left-hand corner), as a winged cherub

to establish them we need to backtrack briefly to the year 1891 when, as already mentioned, he set out with Alexandrine for a sight-seeing tour of the south of France. Their itinerary took in the Pyrenean town of Lourdes where they encountered unexpected difficulty in finding hotel accommodation. Quite unintentionally, they had timed their arrival to coincide with the annual pilgrimage, and Zola was deeply moved by the sight of these crowds of sick and crippled men and women communally uplifted by their faith in the healing power of the Virgin of Lourdes, who had first appeared to a young shepherdess of the region about a quarter of a century earlier. He had, of course, heard about Bernadette Soubirous already but, like the old rationalist and anticlerical that he was, had assumed that the 'national pilgrimages' were simply a publicity stunt concocted by the Roman Catholic Church in order to strengthen its hold over the imagination of the ignorant. The little he saw at Lourdes on this first visit made him wonder about this facile explanation. He was more puzzled than scandalized to discover how, at the end of a century of scepticism and in spite of the steady encroachment of the scientific outlook, so many people still clung to old beliefs in miraculous apparitions and divine intervention. There was a problem here and it occurred to him that to explore it in the way that came most naturally to him—in a work of fiction—would be a challenging task to undertake when, in a couple of years' time, he had finished *Les Rougon-Macquart*.

Accordingly, Zola returned to Lourdes the following summer to make a more thorough investigation and to talk to anyone who could offer him relevant information. The strangest rumours started to gain currency and even credence, to the effect that Zola, following the example of his one-time disciple Huysmans, was about to abjure his freethinking past and seek reconciliation with the Church. When the novel, called simply *Lourdes*, was published in 1894 there was some disappointment and even anger among the faithful, but thanks to the interest that had been whipped up in advance, it was read at least as avidly as any of the *Rougon-Macquart* novels. Long before he finished it, Zola had decided to write two sequels, one of which would be set in Rome and the other in Paris. His hero, a priest assailed by religious doubts, comes to Lourdes in the hope that his tottering faith will be restored. When this fails to happen, he conceives it as his mission to revitalize the Church so that it can play its proper part in solving the pressing problems confronting the modern world; his journey to Rome is undertaken to enlist support for these ideas. Disappointed here too, he finally, in Paris, espouses the gospel of science and social justice.

After his second visit to Lourdes in 1892 Zola had continued his journey through Provence and down the Riviera. At Monte Carlo, on an impulse, he had taken ship to Genoa, and was given an impromptu civic reception by the enthusiastic inhabitants. On his return to France, he told the posse of journalists who nowadays tended to follow him around everywhere that his 'little escapade' had given him 'a taste for Italy. . . . The land of my forefathers has been a delightful revelation to me.'[4] What he did not add, for obvious reasons, was that the recent experience of fatherhood had turned his thoughts back to his own father and his father's origins, about which he knew nothing but a few garbled stories he remembered hearing from his mother.

However, the paramount purpose of his visit to Rome was to 'document himself' for his unwritten novel. The notes he took about what he heard and saw are almost entirely orientated towards the work in progress, and instead of using his own eyes, too often one feels Zola is recording the imagined reactions of his fictional priest, the somewhat priggish and tiresome Abbé Pierre Froment. Only occasionally, as for instance when describing his impressions on first seeing the frescoes in the Sistine Chapel, does Zola strike a genuinely personal note. He may have sensed an affinity between himself and Michelangelo when he wrote of 'the fellow who shuts himself up with so many square metres of empty wall to fill and who starts his enormous enterprise secure in the knowledge that he has the will and the strength to see it through. . . . An enormous work which goes straight to my heart, the sort of thing I have dreamed of all my life.'[5]

On his return journey from Rome Zola made a detour to visit Venice and see the city where his father was born; he met and talked—through an interpreter—with Carlo Zola, the surviving son of his father's elder brother Marco. But Carlo had no very interesting details to communicate concerning the early life of his uncle Francesco, and Emile's curiosity about his father's beginnings and the history of the family remained unsatisfied.

On the whole Mme Zola took more pleasure from this excursion to Italy than her husband did. She found it easier here than in France to bask in his reflected glory, and she could imagine that Roman society was ignorant of the double life he was leading, whereas she was sure that all her friends in Paris knew. After this first visit she returned regularly on her own for several years running; it was an arrangement that allowed the estranged couple a semi-separation acceptable according to the conventions of the time.

Zola was back in Paris, with a bulging file of notes for *Rome*, on 17 December 1894. The French papers were full of reports of the secret military trial of a certain Jewish army captain called Alfred Dreyfus, who had been caught passing on military secrets to the Germans. The verdict, a foregone conclusion, and sentence of exile to a penal colony, were announced on 22 December. Zola found the strident anti-semitism of some sections of the press distinctly distasteful.

18 Ends and Means: the Dreyfus Affair

If Zola had never concerned himself with Dreyfus, his place in the history of French literature, as one of the four major novelists of the nineteenth century, would still be assured. The crucial part he did play in the famous 'Affair' confers on him an additional significance of an altogether different order, and obliges one to bracket him with the handful of other writers, meddlesome clerks or heroes of the pen as they were diversely regarded in their day, that includes such disparate figures as Milton, Voltaire, Byron and Hugo, who interrupted a life of literary activity to throw themselves into a struggle altogether foreign to the normal preoccupations of men of letters. The incidental result was that they came to be revered or reviled, even long after their death, for reasons quite other than those that ordinarily determine the reputations of great writers.

The cause for which Zola emerged from his tranquil study, which made him the butt of hysterical mobs and which for a few months turned him into a solitary exile separated from friends and family, is not one that can be as simply defined as those for which the other writers we have named gave up home, position, or life itself: popular rights, religious tolerance, the freedom of an oppressed nation. Dreyfus himself was not the cause. Zola met Dreyfus only years later and was unimpressed; if all his sacrifices had been made merely in order to rehabilitate this small-minded professional soldier, he might have wondered if the struggle had been worth it. The cause was greater than Dreyfus, but lesser than 'the Truth', which was what Zola supposed it to be when he declared that 'Truth is on the march and nothing will halt it'[1] or that: 'I defended Dreyfus as I defended Manet, because that was where the truth lay.'[2] What he was really fighting for was neither a man, however unjustly used, nor an abstraction, however noble, but a principle: the principle that in a decent, democratic society, good ends cannot be used to excuse bad means, if only because it is usually those who employ the means who decide which ends are good. Only a crazily optimistic observer would say, looking back over the eighty years that have passed since then, that this principle is now generally accepted and applied. But at least we know that, when it is not applied, the democratic ideal is compromised; and it may be that we owe the beginnings of this knowledge to the stand Zola took in 1898.

If one traces back the famous 'Affair' to its starting-point, one does not need to be excessively generous to the army leaders of the time to grant that the ends they were seeking to encompass, given the tensions of the post-war period, were good. The new German Empire, well aware of the strength of revanchism inside France, was anxiously watchful for any sign of warlike preparations on the part of their old enemy, and maintained an efficient intelligence service to gather and evaluate all relevant information. To counter their efforts, the French had set up a separate department of the General Staff, using the cover-name of the 'Statistical Section', with overall responsibility for military security. The Statistical Section appears to have functioned less as an organization for catching foreign spies operating on French soil than as a perfectly legitimate instrument to ensure that no one with access to military secrets should leak them to any of the country's potential enemies.

Such traitors as there might be serving in the French armed forces would most probably try and sell classified information to a member of the diplomatic staff of one of the Triple Alliance powers: Germany, Austria or Italy. Accordingly, the Statistical Section had its own employees posted inside the embassies and in September 1894 one of these, a cleaning woman whose job was to pick up any documents she found in the German military attaché's waste-paper basket, came in with a piece of paper that appeared to have serious implications. Written in French, it

65 Zola among the pilgrims at Lourdes

listed five items of confidential information, which the writer was evidently proposing to make available to the Germans.

The War Minister, General Mercier, was shown this paper (known in the history of the Dreyfus Affair as the *bordereau* or schedule) and ordered an urgent investigation to discover its source. It was assumed, too hastily, that the writer would need to be a member of the General Staff to have access to the items of information listed; and the one officer so placed whose handwriting bore some likeness to that of the *bordereau* was Dreyfus. Moreover, Dreyfus came from a Jewish family, a circumstance which, in the minds of the career officers charged with the inquiry, made it the more likely that he would be guilty of an unpatriotic act. So they had him provisionally arrested and placed in solitary confinement.

As the investigation proceeded, however, the theory that Dreyfus was the traitor became more and more difficult to sustain. The handwriting experts who were called in were not unanimous in attributing the *bordereau* to him. He had an unblemished record; the most meticulous search of his house and belongings had brought to light no incriminating material; and finally, Captain Dreyfus was very well off, lived comfortably within his means, and would hardly have risked a promising career for the sake of the paltry payments the Germans would make him for the rather trivial military secrets he was suspected of wanting to pass on to them.

Unfortunately, while these inquiries were in progress, the popular press had got wind of the affair. One newspaper, *La Libre Parole*, owned by a notorious anti-Semite called Edouard Drumont, printed its own version of the events under a banner headline: 'High Treason. Arrest of the Jewish officer A. Dreyfus.' For the government not to bring Dreyfus to trial after this would have been to court unpopularity. To have brought him to trial and allowed him to be acquitted would have been worse still: its political opponents would be bound to ask why, if treason had been committed, the traitor had not been brought to book. So Dreyfus was charged before a military court, found guilty and sentenced to banishment for life in a penal colony.

It emerged later that the court martial judges were at first very hesitant about conceding the case against Dreyfus, who defended himself calmly and had no trouble in demonstrating the fragility of the prosecutor's case. But Mercier, abetted by Colonel Sandherr, the head of the counter-espionage section, and Major Henry, his second-in-command, were determined to get the verdict they wanted. They produced a 'secret dossier', so secret indeed that it could not be shown to the prisoner or to his defending officer; and this file, later revealed to have been pieced together by Henry from documents relating to earlier cases of espionage, finally tipped the scales against the unfortunate Dreyfus.

The public, knowing nothing of these moves behind the scenes, accepted the verdict unquestioningly, as did Zola, in so far as he gave the matter any thought. There was, after all, no reason to suppose that

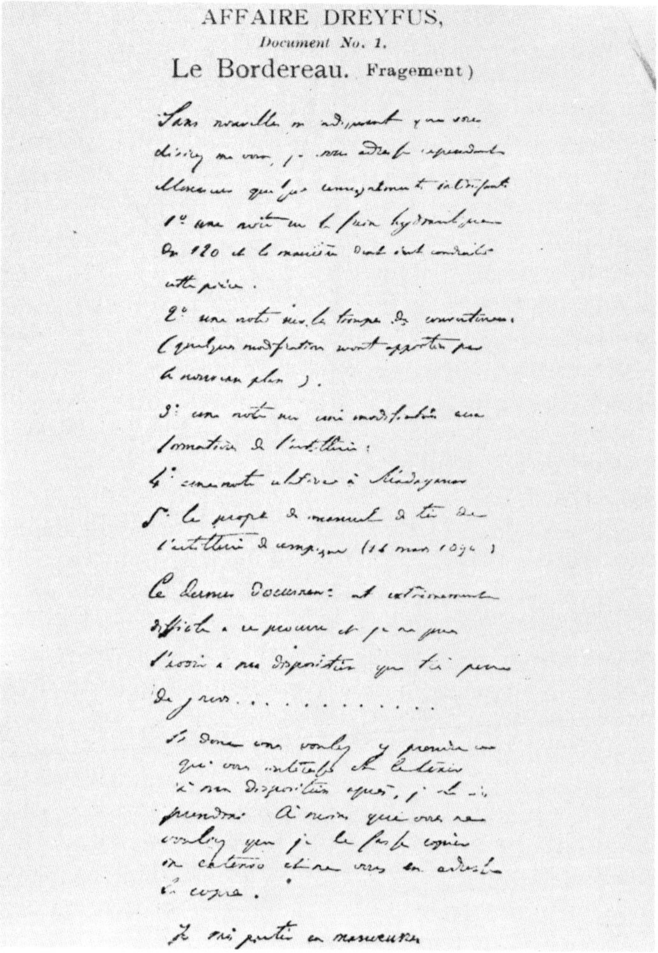
AFFAIRE DREYFUS,
Document No. 1.
Le Bordereau. Fragement)

Sans nouvelles m'indiquant que vous désirez me voir, je vous adresse cependant Monsieur quelques renseignements intéressants
1° une note sur le frein hydraulique du 120 et la manière dont s'est conduite cette pièce.
2° une note sur les troupes de couverture. (quelques modifications seront apportées par le nouveau plan).
3° une note sur une modification aux formations de l'artillerie;
4° une note relative à Madagascar
5° le projet de manuel de tir de l'artillerie de campagne (14 mars 1894)
Ce dernier document est extrêmement difficile à se procurer et je ne puis l'avoir à ma disposition que très peu de jours . . . .
Si donc vous voulez y prendre ce qui vous intéresse et le tenir à ma disposition après, je le prendrai. A moins que vous ne vouliez que je le fasse copier in extenso et ne vous en adresse la copie.
Je vais partir en manœuvres

66 The 'bordereau', written by Esterhazy but originally attributed to Dreyfus, listing five military secrets which the writer was offering to sell to the Germans

Dreyfus was anything but guilty, though it was certainly odd that he kept on proclaiming his innocence, even during the ceremony of public degradation when he was stripped of his badges of rank. But it looked like a purely internal army affair: officers sitting in judgement on a fellow officer. It was reassuring to know they were not prepared to tolerate traitors in their midst. After a few weeks, most people had forgotten Dreyfus's name.

Eighteen months passed by. Colonel Sandherr, who had fallen ill, was removed from the directorship of the Statistical Section and replaced by Picquart, an energetic officer, new to this kind of work, and who had not been involved in the trial of Dreyfus. In March 1896 one of his subordinates brought him a torn-up telegram addressed to a certain Major Esterhazy, of the 74th Infantry Regiment, which seemed to indicate that he too was passing on secret information to foreign powers. Picquart's personal investigations led him to the surprising discovery that Esterhazy's handwriting was identical with that of the famous *bordereau* that had been the principal exhibit at Dreyfus's court martial. Was it possible that a dreadful mistake had been made? To satisfy himself, Picquart went through the records of the trial and to his dismay found that every piece of evidence that had served to destroy Dreyfus could equally well have been used to demonstrate Esterhazy's guilt, if anyone's suspicions had fallen on him. Moreover, Esterhazy, the illegitimate offspring of a famous Hungarian family, had much stronger motives than Dreyfus to betray his country for money: his private life was notoriously disreputable, he was chronically hard up, and he had ruinously expensive tastes.

If, at this point, Picquart's superiors had acted on his discoveries and ordered Esterhazy's arrest, there would have been no Dreyfus Affair. But to take this course of action was impossible without openly admitting that the case against Dreyfus had been trumped up. A number of high-ranking officers would have had red faces or, as they preferred to put it, the country's confidence in the army would have been shaken. Supposing war were to break out when the General Staff itself was implicated in a scandal of such dimensions? The end justifies the means, as the proverb has it. The end, to maintain intact the honour of the army, justified the necessary means: keeping an unimportant Jew in chains on Devil's Island, and silencing the over-zealous Picquart. The forger Henry went to work once more and it was child's play to him to assemble the 'proof' that Picquart— no doubt suborned by Jewish gold—had faked the telegram incriminating Esterhazy. Picquart was sent on a mission to Toulon, from there ordered to Tunis, and finally arrested and unobtrusively incarcerated.

Acting in the best traditions of the service, Picquart forbore to denounce his persecutors, since they were his superior officers, but he did confide his suspicions about the irregularities in Dreyfus's trial to a solicitor friend, Louis Leblois. Though he had no authority from Picquart to do so, Leblois made contact with Scheurer-Kestner, the vice-president of the Senate and a highly respected figure with contacts in government circles. Unfortunately, the steps taken by Scheurer-Kestner to try and get the whole matter properly ventilated merely put the generals on their guard. It was decided that Esterhazy had better be warned and told what to say and what not to say in certain specific circumstances. Thus the General Staff, in their efforts to conceal an earlier mistake, were now forced to enter into a compact with the real traitor who had been selling their secrets all along.

It was when matters had reached this stage, in July 1897, that Zola started taking an interest in the Affair. By now a small nucleus of militants

67 Dreyfus (standing) at the 1894 court martial

had come together, dedicated to rescuing the unfortunate victim of military 'justice'. Led by Mathieu Dreyfus, the prisoner's brother, the group included a certain Bernard Lazare, a young literary critic who had written about Zola, in no very flattering terms, in a collection of essays entitled *Figures contemporaines*. Lazare had also published—abroad—a few pamphlets in defence of Dreyfus; he sent these to Zola, who flicked through them inattentively but gave the author, all the same, a courteous welcome when, a little later, he called on the novelist to find out what his reactions were. Then, in October, Zola received a couple of visits from Leblois, who got him to agree to meet Scheurer-Kestner for lunch. Even then, when all the evidence had been put before him, Zola found it difficult to believe the monstrous story. It still seemed to him a *story*: how were the facts to be disentangled from the fiction? Some of the allegations made by the anti-semitic gutter press—that, for instance, there was a secret syndicate, financed by the Jewish banking community, working to have Dreyfus released—were patently false. But it was equally difficult to believe that Picquart was an innocent man being hounded by the entire General Staff simply because he had unmasked an impudent traitor. Scheurer-Kestner, in pressing for a full and open inquiry, was clearly doing the right thing. Zola wrote three articles, published in *Le Figaro* at the end of November and the beginning of December, in defence of the senator's actions and then, when the editor of the newspaper took fright, continued his campaign with a couple of pamphlets, one directed at the students who had been taken in by anti-semitic propaganda, the other addressed, simply and grandiloquently: 'To France'.

By this time the government had reluctantly decided to accede to Mathieu Dreyfus's public demand that Esterhazy should be tried by a military court for the crime for which his brother had been condemned four years previously. Like all other partisans of Dreyfus, Zola was serenely confident of the outcome, and distressed only by the success the nationalist press was having in playing on the prejudices of the masses:

The case could not be simpler. An officer was found guilty, and nobody questions the good faith of the judges. They condemned him in accordance with their conscience, on the basis of evidence which they believed irrefutable. Then, one day, first one man, then several, begin to have doubts and finally reach the conviction that one piece of evidence, the most important, the only one on which the judges publicly based themselves, was incorrectly attributed to the man found guilty, and that this document is indisputably in the handwriting of another. And they proclaim this, and the other man is denounced by the prisoner's brother, whose strict duty it was to make this denunciation; hence, inevitably, there has to be a fresh trial which is bound, if it ends in a verdict of guilty, to bring about a review of the first case. Is it not all perfectly clear, just and reasonable? In all this, where are the machinations, where is the dark plot to save a traitor's skin? No one denies there is a traitor, all we ask is that the guilty man, not the innocent, should expiate the crime. You will still have your traitor, but it must be the real traitor, that's all.[3]

Thus Zola, speaking with the voice of cool reason. Against this, the gut reaction of those who continued to believe in the end justifying the means was expressed by a journalist called Ernest Renauld who wrote, on the day Esterhazy's trial was ordered (2 January 1898): 'If Dreyfus was innocent, it would be horrible, but it is certain, in the view of successive War Ministers, that he is guilty. And even if he were innocent, is that a reason for shaking the social order to its very foundations?'[4]

Those who had militated on behalf of Dreyfus, Zola among them, had no doubt whatsoever that Esterhazy would be found guilty of the crime of which he was accused. The evidence now marshalled against him was damning. A facsimile of the *bordereau*, set alongside specimens of Esterhazy's handwriting, had appeared in the press; no one could deny the similarity. Some of the letters he had written to his mistress, in which he expressed in the most violent language his hatred of the French, had also been printed. It was unthinkable that he should be acquitted. But the unthinkable happened. On 11 January, without a single dissentient voice, the military tribunal pronounced Esterhazy not guilty of the charges brought against him.

This was the end, or so it seemed. Neither Mathieu Dreyfus, nor Scheurer-Kestner, nor any of their sympathizers had laid plans for this contingency. Zola, too, was thunderstruck, and then, as he said, he felt 'sick with rage'.[5] Anger was an emotion quite foreign to him. There had been moments in the past when he had felt deep sorrow and anguish at the spectacle of some inexcusable injustice, but anger, he had always believed, was a bad counsellor. In this instance, it counselled him well, for it was in a state of controlled fury that he wrote his 'Open Letter to the President of the Republic', which was printed in the newspaper *L'Aurore* on 13 January 1898, under the headline *J'Accuse !*.

In deciding to make his protest not, this time, in the form of a pamphlet, but as an article in the press, Zola had it in mind that the law against libel was much stricter in its application to newspaper comment than to statements made in other publications. He even went so far as to cite, in the text of *J'Accuse !*, the specific articles of the press law of 29 July 1881 under which legal action could be taken against him. He did more than challenge the generals to put him on trial, he made it impossible for them to refuse to do so without dishonour. After giving a clear but detailed account of the Dreyfus Affair from the beginning, Zola went on to name names, accusing this general of culpable negligence, that general of deliberately suppressing evidence, and the War Ministry as a whole of having fomented a press campaign to distract attention from the real issues; and he ended this catalogue with the words: 'Finally, I accuse the first court martial [that which sentenced Dreyfus] of having flouted the law in finding a prisoner guilty on the basis of a document which it kept secret, and I accuse the second court martial [that which white-washed Esterhazy] of having covered up this unlawful act, in accordance with orders received, by committing in its turn the juridical crime of acquitting a prisoner known to be guilty.'[6]

Zola had succeeded in forcing the government's hand: it was impossible for them to ignore *J'Accuse !* without tacitly admitting the justice of the charges he brought. In any case the super-patriots of *La Libre Parole* were howling for his blood. However, the authorities could still, up to a point, choose their ground. Admittedly the case would have to be heard in open court, but with a co-operative judge it might be possible to limit the damage. After due deliberation the Cabinet decided to take proceedings against Zola not for *J'Accuse !* as a whole, but simply for what he had said in the second part of the sentence quoted above: 'I accuse the second court martial of having covered up this unlawful act, in accordance with orders received, by committing in its turn the juridical crime of acquitting a prisoner known to be guilty.' In other words, the court was to hear evidence only on the question whether Esterhazy's trial had been properly conducted. The presiding magistrate was given strict instructions to permit no reference, either by the defending counsel or by the witnesses subpoenaed, to the earlier (1894) trial of Dreyfus. This procedure was facilitated by a peculiarity of French court practice, whereby counsel is not permitted to examine witnesses directly, but must put questions through the judge who reformulates them himself or, if he so decides, may refuse to allow the question.

The trial was fixed for 7 February 1898.

19 Zola on Trial

Zola went into court with few illusions. He could hardly hope for an acquittal; in fact, he was not primarily interested in securing one and urged his counsel, Fernand Labori, to concentrate on seizing every opportunity to throw light on the earlier proceedings against Dreyfus, without troubling himself too much about the defence. He was prepared for a prison sentence and even felt that a quiet cell in Sainte-Pélagie might be a welcome change after the storm unleashed by *J'Accuse !*.

Press accounts of his arrival at the Palais de Justice on the first day of the trial stress the noisy hostility of the waiting crowd. As soon as his carriage was recognized, wrote one reporter, 'a huge roar went up: "Down with Zola! Down with the Jews!"' Zola was described as 'bowed, trembling, deathly pale. He lowered his head as if to make sure the ground was not about to give way beneath his feet.'[1] After that, the police insisted on being told where Zola and his party proposed to lunch each day, and sent two carriages to wait outside the house or restaurant, one to take them to the law courts, the other to accompany them and prevent the crowd from rushing them when they got there. At the end of each session, he and his legal advisers were obliged to spend some time inside the building until the attendants judged it was safe for them to leave. Zola was never allowed to return directly home; he was driven to the house of one friend or another, where he stayed for an hour or so until word reached them that the rowdies waiting for him in front of his house had dispersed.

Inside the court-room, the same menacing atmosphere could be felt, even if its manifestations were subdued. Every vacant seat was taken by anti-Dreyfusards, including a number of army officers in mufti. Zola took little part in the proceedings; he was, as he said, merely a prey over which the lawyers were fighting. For most of the time he felt horribly bored, since nothing was said that he did not already know. He was too cooped up to stretch out his legs and he could not stop fidgeting; as an unfriendly observer noted, 'he nibbles the handle of his cane, rubs the back of his neck, splays or shakes his fingers as pianists do when they are afraid of cramp; he polishes his glasses, swings his left leg up and down, adjusts his collar, stares at the ceiling, twirls his moustache, wrinkles his nose, turns to right and to left . . .'[2]

Except on the rare occasions when he risked a personal intervention—for instance, to protest when the judge refused to permit Dreyfus's wife to testify—Zola was not the centre of attention. His function had, after all, been simply that of a catalyst. The trial had its sensational moments, but

68 Arguments about the Dreyfus Affair were apt to cause dissension even within the most united families. A contemporary cartoon

these were provided by the main actors in the drama. Picquart, who had been brought from prison to take his stand in the witness-box, was the only army officer who refused to be browbeaten by the generals; nothing could stop him telling in his own words the story of how he arrived at his conviction that Esterhazy had been the author of the original *bordereau*. Esterhazy himself, impudently confident that, whatever happened, his superiors would protect him, was overheard saying to a group of civilians in one of the court lobbies: 'They bore me with their *bordereau*. All right, yes, I wrote it! But it was not I who invented it, I was following instructions.' Worried about what he might say in open court, General Pellieux, who had conducted the preliminary investigation before Esterhazy's court martial, forbade him to utter a single word in reply to any question the defence lawyers might put him. Esterhazy objected: 'But General, if those blighters insult me, I can't keep quiet.'—'You will. That's an order.'—'Very well, General.' Albert Clemenceau interrogated him for a full forty minutes, putting to him no fewer than sixty questions about his career, his private life, his financial situation and everything else that might be relevant. Esterhazy, refusing to face the barrister, refusing to answer any of the questions, stood there awkwardly shifting his weight from one leg to the other and twisting his cap in his hands. At the end of the interrogation there came a burst of clapping—for Esterhazy, not for Clemenceau.

The trial ended on 21 February. The verdict went against Zola, as could have been predicted, but the jury was far from unanimous in so concluding, and although the case was lost, the cause was not. In spite of the judge's relentless refusal to allow any questions that might have a bearing on the court martialling of Dreyfus in 1894, certain facts were established which could not but throw grave doubts on the propriety of those earlier proceedings. In the first place, Zola's defence counsel had produced as witnesses a number of experts of unimpeachable standing, palaeographers and professorial members of the Ecole des Chartes, who were shown specimens of Esterhazy's handwriting and asked to comment on the defence's contention that the *bordereau*, which had served to establish Dreyfus's guilt, was in fact the work of Esterhazy. One after the other, they all without exception asserted that only Esterhazy could possibly have drafted the *bordereau*. In the second place, it emerged from the testimony of Edgar Demange, Dreyfus's defending counsel in 1894, that the verdict against his client had been secured by the production of a secret document which he had not been permitted to examine. This was one of the very few occasions when the assize judge did not act swiftly enough to stifle reference to the trial of Dreyfus.

Zola was sentenced to a year's imprisonment and the payment of a fine of 3,000 francs, this being the maximum penalty for the offence. Labori lodged an immediate appeal, which was allowed on a technicality: Billot, the Minister for War, who had brought the case, could not be held to have been libelled in that part of *J'Accuse !* that had been quoted in the charge, for Billot had not, of course, taken any part in the 'second court martial'. The case could only succeed if the court martial judges themselves brought it. The authorities had now to opt between accepting defeat or staging a new trial. They chose the latter alternative but, in order to be sure of a more compliant jury, decided that the case should be heard not in Paris but at Versailles, a small town in which the inhabitants would be less likely to adopt independent attitudes.

The second trial was fixed for 23 May. Extraordinary precautions were taken for Zola's safety. Every movement he made had to be unexpected and unpredictable, so that the gangs of nationalist bully-boys were thrown off the scent; enraged at the thought that the author of *J'Accuse !* was still at large and not behind bars as he deserved, they might well have lynched him if they could have laid hands on him. Desmoulin, who had constituted himself Zola's unofficial bodyguard, went around with a loaded revolver in his pocket.

The plan was to make the short journey from Paris to Versailles by road, so as to avoid the crowds that would certainly have gathered outside the railway station. Zola spent the night of 22 May in the house of a friend of Desmoulin at Saint-Cloud. Here they were picked up by an automobile, at that date a little used and somewhat eccentric mode of conveyance. The drive to the court building at Versailles passed without incident— Zola found the first car ride of his life quite exhilarating—and their arrival went practically unnoticed. As had been foreseen, the demonstrators were all down at the railway station and it was Picquart who, when he got off the train, had to beat off an angry, frustrated mob of right-wing hooligans.

Inside the court-room, the proceedings lasted less than an hour. Labori pleaded that the case could not be heard at Versailles since the alleged offence had been committed in Paris; so the presiding magistrate suspended the sitting until the Appeals Court could pronounce on this new objection. Zola's friends hustled him out of the building and into the motor-car which drove through the gates at high speed, momentarily scattering the demonstrators. As soon as they had recovered from their surprise they set off in hot pursuit, flinging stones at the strange vehicle which, however, travelling at a good thirty miles an hour in the direction of Paris, soon disappeared in a cloud of dust and exhaust fumes.

The Appeals Court found against Labori on this occasion, holding that *L'Aurore*, in which *J'Accuse !* had been published, had certainly circulated outside Paris, so that the alleged offence could be deemed to have been committed as well in Versailles as in Paris. A resumption of the trial was accordingly ordered for 18 July.

This was, for Zola, a long, tiring and desolating day, which began when he left his house in the Rue de Bruxelles at eight in the morning and ended in the small hours as he stood on the deck of a cross-Channel steamer churning away in the direction of Dover. Desmoulin and he drove first to Charpentier's house in the Avenue du Bois de Boulogne where

69   The court room at the first trial (February 1898). Zola can be seen on the left, in the foreground

they breakfasted and then set off in a brougham through the leafy avenues of the Bois and the quiet suburb of Sèvres. At Viroflay they were met by an escort of police cyclists who gave them safe conduct to the gates of the court-house. The atmosphere was much calmer than it had been in May, when the anti-Dreyfus agitation was exacerbated by election fever. In the interval a new parliament had assembled and a new government, led by Henri Brisson, had taken office. Political commentators believed that the strongest man in the cabinet would prove to be Cavaignac, who replaced Billot as War Minister. Godefroy Cavaignac, whose father had organized the suppression of the Paris working-class rising in June 1848, was a man of the right, fair-minded but blinkered. He honestly believed in Dreyfus's guilt, taking to be genuine all the forgeries Henry had added to the Jewish officer's *dossier*; as for the troublesome resemblance between Esterhazy's handwriting and the handwriting on the *bordereau*, he was willing to accept any theory, however implausible—that Dreyfus had cunningly imitated Esterhazy's fist, or that the two men were working in collusion—it didn't matter. What did matter was that the Affair should now be pigeon-holed and the revisionist agitation silenced, but without the use of violence. So the word went out to the military: simmer down, let the law take its course, and soon the whole wretched business will be forgotten.

This was, of course, just what the revisionists feared most. Zola's advisers knew that this case was lost in advance, but so long as it could be kept open, the Affair could be kept alive. Hence Labori's constant efforts to raise every pettifogging objection he could think of to delay the final judgement; and even when he ran out of expedients, there was still one course of action he could fall back on: he and his client would simply leave the court before deliberations were completed and allow judgement to go against them by default. In that case, the normal procedure was for the decision to be notified to the defendant by a process-server; but until that formality had been accomplished the case was not regarded as closed.

For this manoeuvre to succeed it would be necessary to place Zola out of reach of French jurisdiction; in other words, he would have to leave the country that very day, without returning home. Labori accompanied him back to the Charpentiers' house and Desmoulin was dispatched to fetch Mme Zola. Not daring to bring even a suitcase, she tucked a night-shirt and a few other necessities inside a rolled-up newspaper and this was all the luggage Zola left with. A cab was called and husband and wife were hastily bundled inside, Charpentier following in his own carriage. Alexandrine was on the verge of tears; Zola gripped her hand silently. At the Gare du Nord they had the good luck to find an empty first-class compartment just behind the engine. Charpentier and Alexandrine stood on the platform, exchanging a few last words with the reluctant fugitive and trying to make sure he remained hidden from view. Then, with a great snort and puffing of steam, the express for Calais drew off into the gathering darkness.

20 The English Scene

There were a number of reasons why Zola and his friends should have fixed on Great Britain as the country where it would be most prudent for him to settle pending a change in the political situation in France. The United Kingdom was, in the first place, a traditional haven in the nineteenth century for refugees of every political colour: Napoleon III and Eugénie had come here after the collapse of the Second Empire, and so had Vallès and some of his fellow *communards* after the abortive civil war of 1871. Then again, Zola had visited England once already and might, in consequence, feel less lost than in a country totally unknown to him; moreover, he had a few good friends here whose discreet co-operation could be counted on. And finally, communications between Paris and London were excellent.

All the same, Zola's thoughts, as he leaned back in his window seat letting the cool night air ruffle his hair, were anything but cheerful: in the chaos of his emotions a sour rancour predominated. So this was his reward for having had the courage to speak out against injustice and trickery in high places: to be hunted out of the country, torn away from his family, from his work, sent to live among foreigners, forced to keep even his identity secret, perhaps for weeks, perhaps for months. And poor Jeanne, who had no idea as yet . . . Now if he had been twenty years younger, he might have been ready for the adventure, excited by the prospect of a complete break in routine. He recalled, fleetingly, another solitary train journey, when he set out from Marseilles in the middle of the war to go to Bordeaux and look for work. He remembered the anguished parting from Alexandrine then, but their only real worries were about money. And, of course, about the state of the country. The state of the country! Well, it hadn't changed much for the better. The Prussians weren't investing Paris, but there were enemies within, just as dangerous.

At this point in his reflections he suddenly realized he was hungry. He had lunched at Versailles on a bread roll, and at Charpentier's dinner table hadn't been able to swallow a morsel. At Amiens, where there was a five-minute stop, he found the station buffet open and was able to buy a small loaf and a cold leg of chicken. After that he resumed his sombre meditations until, at midnight, the train drew into Calais Maritime. Charpentier had bought him a through ticket to London and since, in those days, travellers between France and England had no need to show passports, he was able to make his way straight on to the ship. There were no more than thirty passengers and not one of them was French, so at least it didn't seem likely he was being followed. The sea was calm, the sky clear, and from the deck where he stood, leaning over the handrail, he watched the twinkling lights of Calais recede and realized that tears were filling his eyes. It had been a long day and he was at breaking-point. Why hadn't they let him go to prison in France?

It was still dark when he disembarked and stumbled into the London train. He felt thirsty now and could have done with a glass of milk, but the effort of making his wants known would have been too great. So he sat in the train, waiting for it to leave, as the sky began to whiten in the east. He had done this journey once before, and he remembered the reception committee, the speech of welcome in French, everyone so friendly. There would be nobody there to meet him this time. He groped in his pocket to find the scrap of paper on which Desmoulin had written the name of the hotel he was to stay at: Grosvenor. Whereabouts would that be? And he had no luggage . . . would they make difficulties about giving him a room? Zola stared out disconsolately on to the Kent fields, peering through the rain. Mesmerized, he fell asleep at last.

He had left Paris when it was still bathing in the warm sunshine of a July evening; London, by contrast, was smothered in a chilly white fog. Zola stepped out of the train and walked over to one of the cabs drawn up for hire, calling out the name of his hotel to the driver sitting up in his box. To his dismay, the man shouted something incomprehensible at him and waved him away. What could be wrong? Zola felt the sweat start to run down his back. In desperation, he pulled open the carriage door and climbed inside, bawling 'Grosvenor' once more. There was a moment's pause, then the cab lurched forward and stopped again. The driver flung open the door and pointed with his whip to the lettering over the hotel doorway. So that was it! Why couldn't Desmoulin have told him that the hotel was in the station precinct?

Zola spent only a couple of nights at the Grosvenor. Having been shown to a gloomy room on the fifth floor, he wrote a hasty note to the only friend in London whose address he had, E. A. Vizetelly; posted that morning, it reached its destination the same evening and the next day a council of war was held, with Desmoulin and Bernard Lazare also present, having travelled over specially from Paris. They lunched in the hotel on what Vizetelly called 'anchoretic fare'—omelets, fried sole, fillet of beef and potatoes—and then repaired to Zola's room to deliberate. Afterwards, leaving Lazare to catch the 2.30 from Charing Cross Station back to Paris, Desmoulin went in search of a competent solicitor to advise them on the legal position, while Vizetelly took Zola off for a stroll in St James's Park.

He had taken the minimal precaution of registering at the Grosvenor under an assumed name. So far, his presence in England had remained undetected, though it was known, of course, that he was no longer in France and, for some reason, Norway was tipped as the country where he was most likely to have taken refuge. But it was obviously dangerous for him to remain in London, where any alert journalist might recognize him; accordingly, on 21 July, the three men, Vizetelly, Zola and Desmoulin, boarded a suburban line train at Waterloo. Seen from the carriage windows, South London appalled Zola; he wondered aloud how the English working classes could be content to live in these mean little cottages, all jammed together, rather than in tall apartment houses as in Paris. But Wimbledon, where they got off the train, delighted him, with its windswept common and the innumerable girl cyclists who seemed to him so much more graceful in the saddle than their French sisters. However, they could not stay here: Wimbledon was not the retired spot Vizetelly had in mind; so they pushed on to Weybridge, where rooms were found for Zola and Desmoulin in the Oatlands Park Hotel.

For the next few days Zola toured the neighbourhood looking at furnished houses to let. The weather had turned fine, and the trim gardens with their splendid holly hedges and huge elms gave him an altogether better impression of the English scene than he had formed hitherto; if only he had his camera with him . . . The local house-agent produced addresses of four desirable properties, but of these only one, a commodious detached villa called Penn, at Oatlands Chase, Walton-on-Thames, took Zola's fancy. Using a different cover-name, he signed an agreement to rent it for four weeks at five guineas a week, the tenancy to run from 1 August. The language difficulty was overcome when Vizetelly sent his sixteen-year-old daughter Violette, who spoke French fluently, to housekeep for him, with a cook-general to help her.

But all Vizetelly's well-meaning efforts could not dispel Zola's feeling of acute homesickness. Although Penn was a well-appointed modern house, there was much about it that made him feel uncomfortable, not least the abominable taste evident in the profusion of hideous china ornaments and in the sentimental prints that covered the walls—dogs looking soulfully into their mistresses' eyes, bright-eyed squirrels cracking nuts, sparrows hopping about in the snow, butterflies flitting from rose to rose. He felt more at home in the garden, among real live robins whose tameness amused him, and where the vegetable plot reminded him of the one at Médan. On the other hand, the way the cook massacred those same vegetables, boiling the taste out of them and serving them up without the slightest dab of butter, horrified him. He asked Violette Vizetelly to tell her to give him only salads in future.

To keep boredom at bay, he needed to get back to some steady routine of work. Desmoulin, on one of his trips, had brought over all the material Zola had assembled for his next novel, *Fécondité*, and once he had sorted out his notes he was able to start on the first chapter. Beginning at ten o'clock in the morning, he wrote steadily for the customary three hours and felt happier when, at the end of it, he was able to put the usual five written sheets into the folder. But after that there was the whole of the rest of the day to get through. At home, he would have had the newspapers to read, letters to open and answer, visitors to receive, the children to see perhaps, a hundred different things to occupy him—but here there was nothing to do but sit and read in his room or in the garden if the weather was warm enough. He asked Vizetelly to lend him some books in French, specifying Stendhal's two major novels and half a dozen titles from Balzac's *Comédie humaine*; they were works he had probably not opened for twenty years, and *La Chartreuse de Parme*, in particular, seemed to him quite extraordinary, fascinating in spite of its faults. The chapters where Stendhal describes Fabrice escaping across the frontier from Parma to Bologna and living in hiding for fear of being thrown into prison if he returned seemed to have a strange prophetic application to his own case and he thought, briefly, of writing an essay on Stendhal to correct some of the unkind things he had said about him in *Les Romanciers naturalistes*.

Then the clouds lifted. On the evening of 11 August the good Vizetelly arrived at his door, bringing with him Jeanne, Denise and Jacques. They had had their share of persecution over the last few months, for Zola's political enemies had not scrupled to ferret out every detail of his private life that could be given a discreditable twist. Reporters discovered the address of the little house in Verneuil-sur-Seine where Jeanne and the children were living and laid siege to it. One sadistic patriot went to the lengths of sending the eight-year-old Denise a letter through the post which was found to contain a photograph of her father with the eyes poked out. They had given their persecutors the slip by stealing out of the house at dead of night and taking a short cut through the woods to the railway station, escorted by a friendly neighbour with a stout stick. The children had been told, in case they let the secret out inadvertently, that they were going to join their father in Russia; consequently it had been a delightful surprise to find themselves crossing the water, until the ship's motion made them feel sick.

Jeanne thought even less well of Penn than Emile did, and when the lease ran out they moved to another furnished house called Summerfield in the neighbouring village of Addlestone. The garden here was much bigger, neglected and overgrown, but the children loved it. In the mild September afternoons Zola sat outside in a wicker chair listening to them at play and struggling to make sense of the news items relating to the Dreyfus Affair in the *Telegraph* and the *Standard*. He had worked his way through an English grammar and Vizetelly had lent him a bilingual edition of *The Vicar of Wakefield*; eventually, with the help of a dictionary, he was able to puzzle out the meaning of a passage of English, though the spoken language remained a mystery to him to the end. He found, however, that the phlegmatic islanders were not in the slightest perturbed by the odd pantomime he resorted to in shops to make his wants known, and were usually able to serve him without too much trouble.

But the school holidays came to an end and then Denise and Jacques

OATLANDS PARK · HOTEL CO., LTD.,
WALTON-ON-THAMES, SURREY. (Postal Address : WEYBRIDGE.)

ONLY 17 MILES FROM WATERLOO STATION (MAIN LINE), LONDON, AND TEN MINUTES' RIDE FROM WALTON OR WEYBRIDGE STATIONS.

Beauchamp Esqr

This beautiful Hotel stands in its own well wooded Park of 40 acres, overlooking the Thames, and contains handsome Suites of Apartments, numerous large and airy Bed-rooms, Coffee and Public Drawing Rooms, Billiard and Smoking Rooms. Table d'hote daily. Lawn Tennis Court. Excellent Stabling, and Horses and Carriages on Hire.

July 1898. A. GRACE, MANAGER.

No. 35

	29			30			31			1													
	£	s.	d.	£	s.	d.	£	s.	d.	£	s.	d.	£	s.	d.	£	s.	d.	£	s.	d.	£	s.
DAILY TOTAL Bt. forwd.				1	11	3	3	4	3	4	14	9											
APARTMENTS		8	6		11			11															
ATTENDANCE		3			3			3															
BREAKFASTS		1	6		1	6		5															
LUNCHEONS		5	6		3			2	6		2												
DINNERS		11			10	6		11															
ALE & STOUT		1				6			6														
SHERRY																							
PORT																							
CHAMPAGNE																							
CLARET					1	6																	
BURGUNDY																							
MOSELLE																							
HOCK																							
SAUTERNE																							
CHABLIS																							
LIQUEURS																							
BRANDY																							

70 Zola's bill from the Oatlands Park Hotel. Note the name given (Beauchamp), one of several pseudonyms he adopted during his stay in England to confuse journalists

had to return with their mother to France. There was no point, once they had gone, in keeping on Summerfield, so he moved into the Queen's Hotel in Upper Norwood where he stayed for the remainder of his time in England. Alexandrine joined him here at the end of October but found the climate more than she could stand; after a few weeks she returned to Paris and Zola spent his one and only English Christmas in far from festive mood. He did, however, cause a considerable sensation in the Upper Norwood Post Office by buying over a hundred 'foreign' (2½d) stamps for all the greetings letters he needed to send abroad.

Although there was no immediate question of his returning to France, the prospects of the revisionist cause began to look distinctly brighter in the New Year. An attempt by the nationalist Déroulède to bring off a *coup d'état* at the funeral of the President of the Republic, Félix Faure, on 23 February ended in farcical failure. A petition for a retrial, made on her husband's behalf by Lucie Dreyfus, was referred to the Appeals Court and Zola made up his mind that, whatever the result, he would return to France and risk the consequences. In fact, on 3 June the court concluded in the petitioner's favour and Zola left by the night train, arriving back in Paris the following morning.

21 A New Century

Zola had left France with a night-shirt and a toilet-bag wrapped up in newspaper; he returned with a stout travelling trunk containing, amongst much else, two life-size china cats—apparently the only items of Victoriana he treasured sufficiently to keep—and the manuscript of *Fécondité* of which he had written the last page on 27 May 1899, only a few days before he packed his bags.

Like *La Terre* and *Lourdes*, it was a novel he had wanted to write for some years before he managed to find time to do so. As early as July 1892—that is, a little less than a year before the last volume of the *Rougon-Macquart* cycle was published—he was telling journalists of his idea for a book about infant mortality; at that time he was thinking of

71 Denise and Jacques having tea with their mother; this photograph may possibly have been taken in the garden of the house in Addlestone which Zola rented when his family joined him in England

175

72 Zola reunited with Jeanne after his return to France

calling it *Le Déchet*, a word which in French has something of the sense of 'criminal waste'. He referred again to this project in an article published four years later in *Le Figaro* on the subject of 'depopulation', a burning question in France at the end of the century. In 1800, according to the best estimates that could be made, the population of France greatly exceeded that of Germany or the British Isles. But the demographic explosion in the first half of the century was much better contained in France than in the rest of Europe, and since approximately 1870 the population had stopped growing, whereas in Germany it continued to rise. This put the French in a poor posture for the ultimate *guerre de revanche*, and also meant that while other European countries were planting settlements overseas—in North America, South Africa, and the recently discovered lands of the South Pacific—the French, apart from colonizing Algeria, were content to stay at home.

Although it may be significant that Zola only started to concern himself with population problems after he had fathered two children himself, his motives for writing *Fécondité* were more likely to have been patriotic than personal. As the idea of this novel matured in his mind, it changed from being a purely negative attack on the evils of abortion, baby-farms, and the (in his view) deplorable practice of contraception, and became trans-figured by his vision of a new France where, as he said at the conclusion of the article on 'depopulation', every married couple would produce a family of twelve children 'to proclaim the joy of humanity under the sun'.[1] In other words, the work he now envisaged was to be prophetic and optimistic, and in these respects would be quite different from his earlier novelistic production.

The utopianism of *Fécondité* understandably disconcerted his critics, more particularly when it became clear that the book was to be only the first of four 'gospels', each one making equally sanguine forecasts of the fuller, healthier, happier and more harmonious society that Zola saw being established in the not-too-distant future. After the publication in 1901 of the second volume in the tetralogy, *Travail*, Vizetelly wrote him a warning letter about the disappointment it had caused in Great Britain, where most reviewers were dismissing it as 'less a work of fiction than a combination of sermon and pamphlet'. 'I have never consulted the tastes of the public,' declared Zola in his reply, 'and I am too old now to modify my work in order to please it. I am writing these books with a certain purpose before me . . . showing what I hold to be wrong and what I think would be right. When I have finished these *Evangiles*, when *Vérité* and *Justice* [the last two volumes in the series] are written, it is quite possible that I shall write shorter and livelier books. Personally I should have everything to gain by doing so, but for the present I am fulfilling a duty which the state of my country imposes on me.'[2]

It is easy to be dismissive about this sudden outbreak of missionary fervour, but to be fair, one must make allowance for the pressures on Zola at this time; the solemnity with which he embarked on his self-appointed mission to regenerate the French nation could be regarded as one of the few regrettable consequences of his embroilment in the Dreyfus Affair. A taunt frequently aimed at him by his political enemies was that he was no true patriot: this half-Italian, hand-in-glove with the rootless Jews, who had denigrated the French fighting man in *La Débâcle* and done his best to corrupt French youth in a dozen other obscene and irreligious produc-tions, was now engaged in sapping the faith of the nation in its military leaders—this was how, by and large, the anti-revisionists presented him in their propaganda. This line of attack forced Zola to re-examine his own feelings towards his native country. True patriotism did not lie, he decided, in the 'my country right or wrong' attitude of the average chauvinist. On the other hand he could not concur with the extreme left-wing view that love of one's country was an outdated tribal instinct which would disappear with the spread of international socialism. He believed that France had an important role to play in the world, but it was

73 Advertisement poster for *Fécondité*, which was serialized in the newspaper *L'Aurore* in 1899

one she had lost sight of or temporarily abnegated. Certain qualities peculiar to the French—their gift for rational analysis and clarity of thought, their sense of order and justice, their belief in individual rights and in the rule of law—these constituted the nation's special contribution to the spiritual treasure-house of mankind; but they were faculties that needed intensive cultivation if they were to bear their proper fruits. This was the message that Zola wanted his *Evangiles* to carry. *Fécondité* pointed the way to a healthier attitude towards family life, *Travail* indicated the path to be followed if reconciliation between the social classes was to be achieved, *Vérité* would be primarily concerned with the reform of French education, while *Justice*—as far as one can tell, for the book was never written—would deal with the problem of militarism and its eventual resolution through planetary federation.

Each of the *Evangiles* was written to the same pattern: an illustrative analysis of the desperately evil situation at present obtaining, followed by an improbably optimistic and lyrically utopian projection into the future, which for Zola meant, of course, the new century which was dawning. The nineteenth century had numerous and undeniable achievements to its credit, in particular in the domain of scientific technology, as was amply demonstrated in the Paris World Fair of 1900 which Zola visited, clicking

74 One of Zola's most effective photographic studies: the Trocadéro Palace (built for the 1878 Exhibition) seen through the arch of the Eiffel Tower (built for the 1889 Exhibition)

75 Photograph by Zola of the Palais de l'Electricité at the 1900 Exhibition

his camera enthusiastically. But it had left unsolved a world of social and moral problems which the twentieth century would have to deal with, and Zola felt triumphantly confident that it would do so. That his life was cut short when it was can be seen almost as a merciful dispensation. Had he lived to the age of eighty, as Wells did, and seen how ill he had guessed the 'shape of things to come', it is possible that he would have succumbed to the same mood of black discouragement as Wells did before he died.

Barring accidents, Zola might have lived to eighty; at sixty, he was in robust good health and still brimful of vitality. Apart from the *Evangile* novels and a series of polemical articles written before and after Dreyfus's second trial at Rennes in 1899, he also found time during these years to exercise his creative talents in a totally new sphere: to the considerable astonishment of the musical public, in February 1897 his name appeared on all the playbills in Paris as the librettist in a new operatic work by Alfred Bruneau called *Messidor*.

Bruneau and Zola had first come together in March 1888, about the same time as Jeanne Rozerot joined the domestic staff at Médan. Bruneau, a struggling composer making a bare livelihood by correcting proofs in the office of a music publisher, called on the novelist to see if he could get his permission to turn *La Faute de l'abbé Mouret* into an opera. Unfortunately, he had been forestalled by Massenet, to whom Zola had already assigned the rights on this particular text; but rather than disappoint Bruneau, for whom he conceived an instant liking, he offered to give him the first refusal of *Le Rêve*, the novel he was currently engaged in writing. Overjoyed, Bruneau accepted; for his librettist he chose Louis Gallet, a poet with previous experience of working with such composers as Bizet, Saint-Saëns and Massenet himself.

Le Rêve was produced at the Opéra-Comique on 18 June 1891. Zola's backstage influence was detectable in the unusual modernism of the costumes; the appearance of the young hero Félicien in workman's overalls created a mild sensation. Musically, however, the work met with the complete approval of the connoisseurs, and in the autumn *Le Rêve* crossed the Channel and was sung at Covent Garden. A couple of years later Bruneau came near to repeating this success with another light opera, *L'Attaque du moulin*, drawn from the story of that title which Zola had published in 1880 in the composite volume *Les Soirées de Médan*. Once again, the libretto was the work of Gallet, though this time Zola collaborated, anonymously and to a minor extent: it is known that he wrote the text of at least one scene, the 'forest farewell'. According to the conventions of the time, the libretto was in verse, as had been that of *Le Rêve*; it was the first time Zola had written any poetry since his rhyming days in the early 1860s.

Delighted by Bruneau's success, he presented him, later the same year, with a libretto of his own composition; this was *Messidor*, written not in rhyming couplets but in rhythmic prose. The use of prose instead of verse was in itself an innovation which gave music critics and composers a lot to argue about, but it was not the only novelty in the opera; choosing an aggressively modern theme, overlaid none the less with Wagnerian symbolism, Zola depicted in *Messidor* the conflict between monopolistic capitalism and the idyllic peasant economy that it displaced. The title itself was meant to recall that of *Germinal*, Zola's novel about industrial strife, Germinal and Messidor both being names of different months in the revolutionary calendar that the First Republic imposed in 1793 in place of the traditional Gregorian calendar.

The second libretto Zola wrote for Bruneau was in the composer's hands even before *Messidor* had its opening performance at the Paris Opera on 19 February 1897. Entitled *L'Ouragan*, it was even more Wagnerian in inspiration than the previous work, though the underlying idea had its roots in Zola's private experiences. He explained the symbolism of the title in his programme notes; it was, he said, 'the hurricane of our passions which, suddenly, without reason, blows across the blue sky of ordinary life, wrecking everything and sweeping everything before it, until the cheerful sun shines again, leaving us devastated, bleeding, to face our life as it starts up again'.[3] At the time he wrote the libretto, the emotional hurricane caused by Alexandrine's discovery of his infidelity had just blown itself out. The plot he devised, turning on the love of two sisters for the same man, is obviously a piece of transposed autobiography. One of the two, Marianne, is domineering and jealous, and must be taken to represent Alexandrine; faced with the loss of Richard's love, she plots to kill him. The other sister, gentle and loving, is called Jeanine; Zola hardly bothered to disguise his mistress's name.

Bruneau began composing the music for *L'Ouragan* before the Dreyfus Affair blew up, and was working on it steadily all the time Zola was living in exile in England; on his return the score was far enough advanced for Bruneau to play it through to him on the piano. It had its opening night on 29 April 1901, and although only twelve performances were given, critics and audiences were deeply moved; the extraordinary way in which music and text complemented one another aroused universal admiration. 'This is really,' wrote Catulle Mendès, 'the work of a single mind, of two minds which by an act of will have turned themselves into one.'[4]

L'Enfant-Roi, the third libretto Zola wrote for Bruneau, has an even stronger autobiographical basis, though the events he dramatized were drawn from a slightly later and calmer period of his life. Setting and story, in contrast to *L'Ouragan*, are modern to the point of banality. A married couple, a baker and his wife, have been unable to have any children; but before she married, the wife had a son by a cousin who was killed on the field of battle. Her husband discovers she is paying secret visits to this child, and his jealousy is aroused. Finally, however, realizing she cannot be happy if separated from the boy, he generously agrees to adopt him. This scenario was an almost exact representation of Zola's own predicament, torn as he was for many years between Alexandrine and the two children Jeanne had given him, until finally his wife agreed to let them visit the house and meet her; though, presumably to spare her feelings, he had covered up the resemblance by inverting the sexes of the two principals, so that it is the heroine who, like Zola, has to conceal the fact that she had a child born outside wedlock, while it is the husband who, like Zola's wife, is at first consumed by jealousy, and later becomes reconciled to the existence of the love-child, 'l'enfant-roi'.

Bruneau completed the score for this opera in August 1902, but only a few weeks later he was horrified to learn that his old friend and collaborator was dead: on the morning of 29 September, Zola's lifeless body was discovered lying on the bedroom floor of his Paris house. Startling rumours of suicide gained temporary currency, but were quashed when it became known that the novelist's death had been caused by inhaling toxic fumes from an open fire in the bedroom hearth. Mme Zola had very nearly shared the same fate; fortunately, when the accident was discovered, she was still breathing though completely unconscious. After she had recovered sufficiently to talk, she was able to tell the police that she remembered waking up in the middle of the night with a violent headache and a feeling of nausea; she had started to walk towards the bathroom when she fell back on the bed. Her husband, hearing her groan, confessed he felt sick too. Alexandrine wanted to ring for help, but he told her not to disturb the staff unnecessarily. In fact, for a fortnight or so previously Zola had been waking up each night, feeling as though he was suffocating, after a dreadful nightmare in which he saw Alexandrine and himself writhing in a fiery furnace and perishing miserably.

The autopsy and subsequent inquest showed that death was due to carbon monoxide poisoning. A fire had been lit in the bedroom grate, on Zola's instructions, the previous evening; a common type of smokeless fuel was used, but the fumes had evidently not been carried up the chimney. Instead, they had collected at ground level and Zola, having fallen on the floor, would have been unable to escape the toxic effects whereas his wife, lying on top of the high bed, was lucky enough to survive till the morning.

A verdict of accidental death was accordingly brought in and nobody thought to challenge it, in spite of the obvious difficulty of explaining how the forced draught up the flue had failed to carry away the coal-gas. The possibility that the chimney had been deliberately sealed was mooted only years later and in consequence of an alleged death-bed confession on the part of a workman employed at the time of Zola's death to carry out certain repairs on the roof of the adjoining house. This man was said to have unburdened his conscience, twenty-five years after the event, to a close friend who himself waited another twenty-five years before breathing a word about it. The story was that he and his mates, hearing from servants' gossip that the hated defender of Dreyfus was due back from the country on one particular evening, blocked his bedroom chimney with rubble and returned early the following morning to clear the obstruction and thus remove all traces of their crime. Though there is nothing inherently improbable in this version of the events, the degree of hearsay evidence, uncorroborated testimony and unverifiable assertion is such that doubt is bound to persist as to the exact circumstances in which Zola met his death.

He had never taken the legal steps necessary to give his children a claim on his estate, which therefore passed in entirety to his widow; its most valuable part was neither his considerable cash deposits at the bank, nor the property at Médan, but the royalties which would continue to be paid, for the next fifty years at least, on his novels. However, he had given Jeanne a document to be shown to his wife in the event of his dying first, in which Alexandrine was asked to ensure that at her own death the property should pass to his two children. She did more than simply comply with this injunction: for the rest of her life she paid each of them an annual allowance of 2,000 francs and also arranged for them to have the right to bear the hyphenated surname Emile-Zola. Thus, at her death in 1925 Denise and Jacques became joint heirs to the family property, which included a mass of documentary and iconographic material relating to their father's private life, not all of which has even now been published. The estate at Médan had, some time before, been turned into an orphanage by Mme Zola in pious memory of her husband, and still serves that function today.

It is not unusual for the reputation of a writer to suffer some eclipse during the first few decades following his death, and Zola was to prove no exception to this rule. His popularity among the mass of the reading public underwent no serious decline, to judge by the sales figures released from time to time by his publishers, but in the inter-war years, with Proust, Mauriac, Julien Green and Roger Martin du Gard in the ascendant, Zola appeared boringly old-fashioned to the intellectual élite. Gide complained about this in 1932: 'I regard the discredit into which Zola has fallen as a monstrous injustice, which reflects poorly on modern literary criticism. There is no more personal and more representative French novelist.'[5] But, having recorded this opinion in his diary, Gide left it at that, and no one else came along to remedy the 'monstrous injustice'. One might have expected the hundredth anniversary of Zola's birth to have occasioned some interesting reassessments, but as ill luck would have it, this centenary fell in the first year of the Nazi occupation of France; and for the Nazis, Zola the 'Jew-lover' was nothing but a degenerate Bolshevist pornographer.

Only in 1952, fifty years after his death, were there clear signs of a change of attitude. It was then that, for the first time ever, one of Zola's novels, *La Terre*, was made the subject of a French state doctoral thesis, and this work of painstaking scholarship helped to promote an intensive research effort led, however, predominantly by American, not French, academics. The 1960s saw the appearance of the first properly annotated editions of the works, the five-volume Pléiade edition of *Les Rougon-Macquart* (recently supplemented by a volume of the collected short stories), and the Tchou edition of the complete works in fifteen massive tomes. The new school of structuralist critics have discovered in Zola an admirable subject for their particular exegetical approach, and anyone who attends, these days, one of the international colloquia organized for students of the naturalist novel may sometimes be tempted to speculate, as he listens to some of the more esoteric and jargon-ridden papers, what the ghost of Zola, if one may suppose so obdurate a materialist to have been granted any form of spectral survival, would make of the mind-boggling manifestations of modern academic appraisal. Would he be gratified, or would his sturdy good sense cause him to recoil in horrified amazement and flit back to whatever Elysian fields he now roams ?

But apart from this no longer very recent resurgence of specialist interest, there remains the heartening persistence of Zola's popularity with the ordinary reader, shown not only in the lists of paperback reprints of his novels sold in France, but abroad too, in the English-speaking world, in the stream of new translations which have been issued over the past twenty-five years. Immediately after the last war, the only work of Zola's available in this country was an Everyman reprint of Havelock Ellis's pedestrian translation of *Germinal*. Today, there is not one of the major novels in the *Rougon-Macquart* series that cannot be read in a competent, often masterly modern rendering. In North America, Zola has always been held in higher esteem than elsewhere, thanks in the first instance to the early critical essays of Henry James and W. D. Howells. His imitators in the United States—Frank Norris, Theodore Dreiser, Stephen Crane, Upton Sinclair—have been more numerous than in any other country, even if none of them, perhaps, ranks as a writer of the very first order. So there is a certain appropriateness in the fact that, today, the principal centre of Zola studies is situated on the other side of the Atlantic, in Toronto, and that the enormous task of collecting, collating and publishing Zola's voluminous correspondence is being undertaken by a joint Franco-Canadian team of scholars to which several outstanding specialists from the United States have attached themselves. When, some time towards the end of this century, they have completed their task and made available the fruits of their labours, the material at the disposal of future biographers will be immeasurably greater and this particular biography will doubtless need to be replaced by a more detailed assessment of Emile Zola and his achievements.

76 The delegation of miners at Zola's funeral, paying a last homage to the author of *Germinal*

Notes

The following abbreviations have been used:

O.C. Emile Zola, *Œuvres complètes*, ed. Henri Mitterand (Paris: Cercle du Livre Précieux), 15 vols., 1966–9.

R.-M. Emile Zola, *Les Rougon-Macquart*, ed. Henri Mitterand (Paris: Bibliothèque de la Pléiade), 5 vols., 1960–7.

Introduction
1. *R.-M.* III, 1825
2. *R.-M.* IV, 1717

1 Father and Son
1. 'In the Days of my Youth', *The Bookman*, December 1901, p. 343
2. *O.C.* XIV, 1035 ('François Zola', in *La Vérité en marche*)
3. Quoted in R. Ternois, 'Les Zola, histoire d'une famille vénitienne', *Les Cahiers naturalistes*, no. 18 (1961), p. 61

2 Aix-en-Provence
1. 'In the Days of my Youth', p. 344
2. *O.C.* IX, 896 (*Le Petit Journal*, 1 June 1865)
3. *O.C.* XIV, 308 ('La Jeunesse française contemporaine')
4. *R.-M.* I, 6 (*La Fortune des Rougon*, chap. I)
5. *O.C.* IX, 441 ('Souvenirs XII', in *Nouveaux Contes à Ninon*)
6. *O.C.* XIV, 1254 (letter dated 10 August 1860)
7. *R.-M.* I, 15 (*La Fortune des Rougon*, chap. I)
8. *R.-M.* I, 1545 (*La Fortune des Rougon*, notes)

3 Lost Illusions
1. *O.C.* IX, 614 ('Aux champs', in *Le Capitaine Burle*)
2. *O.C.* IX, 909 ('Printemps. Journal d'un convalescent')
3. *O.C.* XIV, 1256 (undated letter, September 1860)
4. *O.C.* XIV, 1263 (letter dated 31 October 1860)
5. 'In the Days of my Youth', p. 346
6. Ibid., p. 347
7. *O.C.* XIV, 1300–1 (letter dated 20 January 1862)

4 Cézanne and Gabrielle
1. *O.C.* XIV, 1297 (undated letter, August 1861)
2. *O.C.* XIV, 1287–8 (letter dated 10 June 1861)
3. *R.-M.* IV, 127–8 (*L'Œuvre*, chap. V)

5 The Publishing Business
1. *O.C.* XIV, 1318 (letter dated 24 September 1865)
2. *O.C.* XIV, 1316 (letter dated 6 February 1865)
3. Vallès, *Littérature et révolution*, ed. R. Bellet (Paris, 1969), pp. 393–4

4. Ibid., pp. 140–1
5. Quoted in J. C. Lapp, 'The Critical Reception of Zola's *Confession de Claude*', *Modern Language Notes*, November 1953, pp. 459–60
6. *O.C.* XIV, 1319 (letter dated 8 January 1866)
7. Quoted in G. Vauthier, 'Emile Zola et *la Confession de Claude*', *La Révolution de 1848*, October 1925, pp. 626–30

6 THE ART CRITIC
1. *O.C.* XIV, 328 ('La Jeunesse française contemporaine')
2. *O.C.* XII, 789 ('Le Jury', in *Mon Salon*)
3. *O.C.* XII, 808 ('Les Réalistes au Salon', in *Mon Salon*)
4. *O.C.* XII, 817–18 ('Adieux d'un critique d'art', in *Mon Salon*)

7 ZOLA AND MANET
1. *R.-M.* V, 228 (*L'Argent*, chap. VIII)
2. *O.C.* XI, 506 ('La Féerie et l'Opérette', in *Le Naturalisme au théâtre*)
3. *O.C.* XIV, 1333 (letter dated 29 May 1867)
4. *O.C.* XIV, 1332 (letter dated 29 May 1867)
5. *O.C.* I, 674–5 ('La Littérature putride', in *Le Figaro*, 23 January 1868)

8 BEGINNINGS AND ENDINGS
1. *O.C.* XIV, 1333 (letter dated 29 May 1867)
2. *O.C.* X, 925 (*Le Rappel*, 13 May 1870)
3. Ellis, *Affirmations* (London, 1898), p. 138
4. *R.-M.* V, 1757–8 ('Documents et plans préparatoires')
5. *O.C.* XIV, 1354 (letter dated 22 August 1870)
6. *O.C.* XIV, 1356 (letter dated 7 December 1870)
7. P. Alexis, *Emile Zola, notes d'un ami* (Paris, 1882), p. 173
8. *O.C.* XIV, 1360–1 (letter dated 15 December 1870)

9 FROM THE COMMUNE TO L'ASSOMMOIR
1. *Le Sémaphore*, 3 June 1871. Quoted in R. Walter, 'Zola et la Commune: un exil volontaire', *Les Cahiers naturalistes*, no. 43 (1972), p. 34
2. *Le Sémaphore*, 17 August 1871; quoted in R. Ripoll, 'Zola et les communards', *Europe*, nos. 468–9 (1968), p. 18
3. A. Brisson, *L'Envers de la gloire. Enquêtes et documents inédits* (Paris, 1904), p. 93
4. E. Bergerat, *Souvenirs d'un enfant de Paris. Les années de bohème* (Paris, 1911), p. 400
5. *O.C.* XIV, 1388 (letter dated 24 July 1876)
6. Flaubert, *Correspondance, 4e série* (Paris, 1910), p. 228

10 FRIENDS AND DISCIPLES
1. Mrs M. A. Belloc Lowndes, *Where Love and Friendship dwelt* (London, 1943), p. 182
2. *O.C.* X, 971 (*La Cloche*, 8 November 1872)
3. E. and J. de Goncourt, *Journal. Mémoires de la vie littéraire*, ed. R. Ricatte (Monaco, 1956), VIII, 154–5
4. *O.C.* XI, 137 ('Flaubert. L'Homme', in *Les Romanciers naturalistes*)
5. M. K. Lemke, *M. M. Stassyulevitch i yego sovremenniki v ikh perepiske* (St Petersburg, 1912), III, 48

6. Ibid., 608
7. Goncourt, *Journal*, X, 171
8. Ibid., XI, 90, 178
9. A. Antoine, *Mes souvenirs sur le Théâtre Antoine et sur l'Odéon* (Paris, 1928), p. 180
10. A. Albalat, *Gustave Flaubert et ses amis* (Paris, 1927), pp. 226–7

11 THE LURE OF THE STAGE
1. *O.C.* XII, 303 ('Victor Hugo', in *Documents littéraires*)
2. F. Xau, *Emile Zola* (Paris, 1880), p. 56
3. *O.C.* X, 1209 ('Lettre à la jeunesse', in *Le Roman expérimental*)
4. *O.C.* XV, 123
5. *O.C.* XV, 228 (preface to *Les Héritiers Rabourdin*)
6. Goncourt, *Journal*, XI, 192
7. Shaw, *Prefaces* (London, 1934), p. 217
8. *O.C.* XV, 788 ('*L'Assommoir* au théâtre')
9. Interview with Gaston Calmette, *Le Figaro*, 19 February 1887. Quoted in L. A. Carter, *Zola and the Theater* (New Haven, 1963), p. 128

12 PORTRAIT OF THE MAN
1. Goncourt, *Journal*, XXII, 49
2. Vizetelly, 'Some Recollections of Emile Zola', *Pall Mall Magazine*, vol. XXIX (1903), p. 63
3. Goncourt, *Journal*, XIII, 25
4. A. Antoine, *Mes souvenirs sur le Théâtre-Libre* (Paris, 1921), p. 102
5. Jourdain, 'Zola outragé et calomnié', in *Présence de Zola* (Paris, 1953), pp. 131–9
6. Sherard, *Twenty Years in Paris* (London, 1905), pp. 463–4
7. Bergerat, *Souvenirs d'un enfant de Paris* (Paris, 1911), p. 400
8. Rod, 'The Place of Emile Zola in Literature', *Contemporary Review*, November 1902, p. 623
9. A. Kerr, 'La Maison de Zola', *Nouvelles littéraires*, 8 October 1932
10. *Vingt messages inédits de Zola à Céard*, ed. A. J. Salvan (Providence, R.I., 1961), p. 11
11. *Lettres inédites à Henry Céard*, ed. A. J. Salvan (Providence, R.I., 1959), p. 37
12. *O.C.* XIV, 1286 (letter dated 10 June 1861)
13. *O.C.* XII, 708
14. Ibid.

13 PORTRAIT OF THE WRITER
1. *R.-M.* IV, 1509
2. *R.-M.* III, 1679
3. *R.-M.* II, 1665
4. 'Some Recollections of Emile Zola', *Pall Mall Magazine*, vol. XXIX (1903), pp. 63–5
5. *O.C.* XIV, 800 ('Les Droits du romancier' in *Nouvelle Campagne*)

14 ZOLA AND THE IMPRESSIONISTS
1. *O.C.* XII, 971 ('Salon de 1876')
2. *O.C.* XII, 1018 ('Le Naturalisme au Salon')

15 JEANNE
1. F. Xau, *Emile Zola* (Paris, 1880), p. 49
2. Interview published in *Le Matin*, 7 March 1885, quoted in G. Robert, *La Terre d'Emile Zola, étude historique et critique* (Paris, 1952), p. 127
3. *R.-M.* IV, 1527
4. Ibid.
5. *O.C.* XIV, 733 ('Le Crapaud', in *Nouvelle Campagne*)
6. *R.-M.* IV, 1625–6
7. Goncourt, *Journal*, XV, 177
8. Ibid., p. 89

16 A DOUBLE LIFE
1. Goncourt, *Journal*, XVI, 10
2. *O.C.* XIV, 1469 (letter dated 6 March 1889)
3. *O.C.* XIV, 1472 (letter dated 27 August 1889)
4. Quoted in A. J. Salvan, 'Quatre lettres de Zola à sa femme', *Les Cahiers naturalistes*, no. 41 (1971), p. 77

17 LONDON, LOURDES AND ROME
1. Quoted in E. A. Vizetelly, *Emile Zola, Novelist and Reformer* (London, 1904), p. 265
2. Ibid
3. Ibid., pp. 333–4
4. Quoted in R. Ternois, *Zola et son temps. Lourdes, Rome, Paris* (Paris, 1961), p. 247
5. *O.C.* VII, 1071 ('Rome. Journal de voyage')

18 ENDS AND MEANS. THE DREYFUS AFFAIR
1. *O.C.* XIV, 888 ('M. Scheurer-Kestner', in *La Vérité en marche*)
2. Quoted in L. Deffoux, 'Le Cinquantenaire des *Soirées de Médan*', *Mercure de France*, 15 May 1930, p. 247
3. *O.C.* XIV, 904 ('Lettre à la jeunesse', in *La Vérité en marche*)
4. Quoted by C. Roy, introduction to *La Vérité en marche*, *O.C.* XIV, 866
5. *O.C.* XIV, 1548 ('Notes inédites sur l'Affaire Dreyfus')
6. *O.C.* XIV, 930 ('J'Accuse!', in *La Vérité en marche*)

19 ZOLA ON TRIAL
1. Quoted by H. Guillemin, *Eclaircissements* (Paris, 1961), p. 275
2. Ibid., p. 278

21 A NEW CENTURY
1. *O.C.* XIV, 790 ('Dépopulation', in *Nouvelle Campagne*)
2. Quoted by Vizetelly, *Emile Zola, Novelist and Reformer* (London, 1904), p. 498
3. *O.C.* XV, 672
4. Quoted by F. Robert, introduction to *Pièces lyriques*, *O.C.* XV, 529
5. Gide, *Journal*, 17 July 1932

Index